NOW WHAT

NOW WHAT

Michael D. Goldsmith

CONTENTS

CHAPTER 1

The Right Stuff

It was 5:00 A.M. The alarm was sounding like a bullhorn going off in his room. Josh looked out his window. Last night, he had graduated from med school and was looking forward to what life had in store. Then his mind went back to Vietnam. He could see the rice paddy, and hear his men's screaming going through his ears as if it were happening right below him. He was receiving his degree that day and would become the doctor he wished he had been when his men were dying in that paddy, yet he felt a sense of guilt. Why did he survive and some of his men did not?

After his two-year stint in "Nam," he decided to go into medicine. He had seen men die in the rice paddies. His mind kept wandering back to the day when he and his men were surrounded by North Vietnamese. He could still remember the bullet going into his side. He remembered waking up in a "chopper" as he was airlifted to the evac hospital. When he woke up after surgery, the nurse looking over him smiled.

"Lieutenant, you're going home."

"What?" Josh asked.

"You're going home."

Then he felt a pain in his foot. He tried to move it, but nothing happened. He looked down. His foot was gone. There was a stump where his foot had been.

"Nurse, I was shot in the side. Where did my foot go?" he asked.

"They tell me when you took the bullet, you stepped back and stepped on a land mine. It took your foot. It's amazing what they can do with prosthetics today. Let me tell ya, soldier—God was looking out for ya."

A spark went off in his head. The anger welled up within him. "How could God let this happen? How could a loving God allow such a terrible thing like this damn war to go on killing a bunch of innocent kids on both sides for no apparent reason?"

Sharon, the cute young nurse who was taking care of Josh, knew that this had to be handled directly. She walked over to him, went nose to nose with him, and said one word: "Sin." Then she stepped back.

"What?" Josh asked.

"Sin," Sharon answered. "It's like this. Man, sinned way back in the Garden of Eden. We have had to live with sin ever since, when Cain killed Abel. It all started then. God sent his Son to redeem us from that sin. The problem is this. Man wants to be in control. Man wants to have other men under their thumb to be able to control them."

Josh rolled over. He refused to look at Sharon anymore that day. He had a great deal to go over in his mind. He had grown up in a little Lutheran church. Everyone knew how to act in church, but God— through his Son, by his Spirit—being active in a man's life? Not so much. It just had not sunk in. Sure, they celebrated Christmas and all that stuff, but he had always thought it was just some kind of story. He had never thought about the ramifications of the whole thing. Sure, he was aware of the sin in his own life, yet he had never thought of the macro sin and its result on the world.

The next day, his sergeant came to see him. Sgt. Bruce Johnson stood six-foot-two, a mountain of a man. He took no guff from anyone, yet he had a warm spot for all the men under his command.

He walked in and saw Josh with one foot missing. He smiled and shook his head. "Sir looks like you are going home. I expect that you will start running again in about a year."

Josh got a totally blank look on his face. "Running again?

Sarge, how in God's green earth am I supposed to run on only one foot?"

"A fake foot. Yup, I have seen some guys running some amazing races with those prosthetic limbs. Usually, they have both feet gone. Maybe a bit more interesting with just one. Maybe they ought to cut your other foot off as well."

Anger started to well up in Josh. "How in God's name can you suggest such a thing? Are you making fun of me?"

Bruce shook his head. "Not at all. There is a passage in Romans 8:28, to be exact. 'All things work together for the good for those who love God and are called according to his purpose. I can see God all over this. Look, you were raised in the church. But have you ever really had a close, intimate relationship with the living Christ?"

"Sarge, you are the second person to ask me that type of question. I always believed in answering a direct question directly. No, I have not."

Bruce looked directly into Josh's eyes. "You better give it some serious thought. Jesus wants to use you. You can lie in a bed and mope or get ready to do battle with him who wants to destroy not only your body but your soul and spirit as well in hell."

The weeks following would be tough for Josh. Physical therapy would be excruciating. His side was healing nicely, but his foot—or lack thereof—was causing him all sorts of problems. He had seen runners with no feet winning races, yet with only one foot and one prosthesis, that could really be a challenge.

Then his wife of twelve years snapped him back to the present.

"Josh! What are you thinking about? It seems that you are off in space somewhere," Sharon asked as she touched his shoulder.

"Sharon, I have finished eight years of medical school. I have my MD. Yet those words of Sergeant Johnson keep coming back to haunt me. He told me I should start running races. My mind was going over how I could run such a race with only one real foot and one prosthetic. I have seen guys run races and win with both feet gone—but never one. How am I supposed to do that?" Those words never left his mind.

Sharon smiled at him as she said. "Josh, he could have been talking about Hebrews 12:1–3, which says, 'Therefore, since we are surrounded by such a great cloud of witnesses, let us throw off everything that hinders and the sin that so easily entangles. And let us run with perseverance the race marked out for us, fixing our eyes on Jesus, the pioneer and perfecter of faith. For the joy set before him, he endured the cross, scorning its shame, and sat down at the right hand of the throne of God. Consider him who endured such opposition from sinners so that you will not grow weary and lose heart.' My dear, we are all given a race to run. You have been running yours and overcoming every challenge. The question I have for you is this. What does our father in heaven— through his

Son Jesus, by his Spirit—want you to do with your degree? That is the race that is set before you. Run the race."

"Sharon, this, I do know—I don't think that was what he had on his mind. Sergeant Johnson is a huge believer in Christ. But I really think he expects me to run again."

Sharon got a huge smile on her face. "Well, bucko, you better get ready to run. You have told me that in high school, you were a distance runner, right?"

"That is correct," he answered. Then he continued, "Well, I think for whatever reason, God wants me running again. I don't know how it will work with medicine, but it will."

The twinkle in Sharon's eyes told him she knew all along what the answer would be. She understood that God the Father had already set his mind on doing something remarkable with Sam. If she knew anything about Sam, it was that he did not know the word quit.

Josh got a blank look on his face. "Sam?"

Sharon chuckled a bit. "You know, the young man who was carrying you out. You know he hit a mine, lost both legs at the hip. He won't quit either. You need to take a lesson from him. Don't quit."

Her mind went back to a story he had told her when he was getting his strength back in the hospital. It was a story of being surrounded by the Viet Cong. The mortar shells were blowing up all around them. His men were crying in fear. Josh got control of his men. He got them to get control of themselves. He then proceeded to call in an airstrike. After the strike, he yelled for his men to move out. They would conquer the VC that day. That day would, however, cost Josh his foot and Sam his legs.

"What are you thinking about, babes?" Josh asked.

Sharon looked directly at Josh. "The story you told me about being surrounded by the VC. Does that still affect you today?"

Josh started to choke up. "Yeah, I think it does. That whole damn war does. I can still see my men dying on that paddy. They died for no reason except for a bunch of military armament manufacturers to make their blood money. I have no problem with fighting a war where our country is attacked or threatened. North Vietnam was no threat to anyone—except maybe the south."

Sharon got a concerned look on her face. "Babes, I am thinking of our family. How is this unforgiveness you have toward the people we had in power going to affect your relationship with our kids?" She got up and crossed the room, pulled the Bible off the shelf, and opened it to the Lord's Prayer. "Ah, here it is. 'Forgive us our sins as we forgive those who have sinned against us.' We pray this prayer a great deal. How do you expect God to forgive you when you are holding so much in against this country?"

The sudden rage that exploded hit Sharon like a ton of bricks. The language that Josh used caught Sharon way off guard. She got up, turned, and ran into the bedroom crying.

Josh dropped into the chair, dropped his head in his hands, and cried like a baby. "What is wrong with me? What caused this? Sharon is the love of my life, yet this rage, I don't understand it. She simply stated truth to me. There was no reason for such rage. What is wrong with me?"

In the bathroom, Sharon was weeping as she prayed. "Father, what is going on here? I have never seen such rage from Josh. What can I do?"

She heard a knock at the door.

"Babes, I am so sorry. It hit me like a ton of bricks, and I lost it. I don't know what's wrong with me. Help me, please."

Sharon opened the door slowly. She stepped out and looked at the tears running down Josh's face.

She put her arms around him and said, "Josh, I think there is one person who can help. When you were in the hospital, your sergeant, Bruce Johnson, came in and visited you. He seemed to be a real man of God. I know that was a few years ago. But there must be some way of getting a hold of him."

"Babes, I have no idea how we could get in touch with Sarge but let me try this."

He picked up the phone and dialed the "unit" headquarters.

"Hello, this is Lt. Josh Henderson. I am looking for a Sgt. Bruce Johnson who served in Nam with me during the Tet

Offensive. Can you help me?" Josh asked.

The sweet lady on the other end said, "Let me do some checking. May I get back to you?"

"That would be great," Josh answered. He hung up the phone, turned to Sharon, and said, "Well, babes, which ended that. When they tell a guy, they will get back to them. That's the end. Never a word comes back."

Three months later, Josh was sitting at his desk. His phone rang.

"Hello. Josh here."

The voice on the other end was quite familiar. "Bruce Johnson here. How are you, Josh?"

"Doing well. No, let me restate that. I am having troubles I don't know how to deal with. I would use an expletive to describe it, but I try not to use such language anymore."

"What's the problem, bro?" Bruce asked.

"Bruce, there is a quiet rage under the surface. I don't know what to do with it. Help!"

Bruce looked to heaven and quietly prayed. *Lord, help me. Give me the words for this guy.* "Josh, this country has fought many wars. The problem was this war was fought over money. Not money that any country had taken from us. It was fought so that weapon companies in this country could make billions of dollars off the blood and treasure of this country's young men. We could have won that war, but that's not what we were there for. We lost over fifty thousand men. We also have thousands and thousands of men who are messed up. The problems tend to lie dormant for years and years and then hit the guys like a hurricane. Let's get together and talk this out. I can fly your way and be there next week. Would that work for you?"

"That would work for me. Call when you get in. I can pick you up at the airport, or we can just meet for coffee someplace," Josh answered. It was 7:00 a.m. on Wednesday, the twenty-third. Josh had just brought Sharon her coffee before she could get out of bed. He was sitting on the side of their bed, looking at those beautiful blue eyes God the Father had gifted to Sharon. The phone rang.

"Mornin'. Josh here."

"Morning, Josh. Bruce here. I have some business to take care of in your city today. Would ten at the Buckle work for you?"

"See you there." Josh hung up the phone, looked at his beautiful bride, kissed her on the forehead, and said, "Babes, I better hit the shower. I have a feeling those demons I have from that war are about to be kicked out. I gotta hit the shower."

With that, he got up and headed for the bathroom to get ready for the day.

CHAPTER 2

All Things New

Josh came out of the shower, threw on his jeans, kissed Sharon goodbye, walked to the garage, put his helmet on, put the key in the ignition, started his bike, and rode down the driveway. As he rode along, the beauty of the day struck him with a softness that he would never be able to put into words. As he rode into the parking lot of the Buckle, he spotted Bruce getting out of his car.

"Bruce! Morning!"

Bruce, smiling as he saw his old friend for the first time in years, came over and gave him a man hug with the customary two fist beats on the back. "It's so good to see you, friend. We do have a lot of catching up to do."

Josh smiled. "Man, do we ever."

He reached down, grabbed the door, and waved Bruce in

before him. They were escorted to the table they would be seated at. The waitress would bring coffee with a bright smile. They sat making small talk while they waited on their food. Then Bruce would ask a question that would catch Josh totally off guard.

Bruce leaned across the table, looked directly into Josh's eyes, and asked, "Josh, are you living the beatitudes?"

"What?" was the answer that popped out of Josh's mouth.

"Are you living the beatitudes?" Bruce asked again.

"I have never even thought of them," Josh answered.

Bruce smiled and then said, "You see, most people, when they think of the beatitudes, don't think about what Christ was really talking about. I think people miss the call on us that comes from each of the blessed people who are named in them. The key to the whole thing is this. Do you see a person in mourning? The scripture says they shall be comforted. The question that should come to mind is this. Are we willing to be the one the Father in heaven uses to do the comforting? You see, there are two people with each beatitude. We each have a part in them."

Bruce leaned across the table. "Look, my friend, it's like this. We both saw the same 'crap' in Nam. We survived it. To some extent, there is guilt on us both because we came home. A great number of good men did not. We can do one of two things. We can go inward and be angry with the world because of what happened, or we can start living the beatitudes. When we live the beatitudes, we start looking beyond ourselves. We start looking to see what we can do to help other people. As we look at each of the 'blessed' statements, we see, in many cases, hurting people. I am correct, am I not, that you are went into medicine? There are many reasons people go into that field. One is that they have a desire to help people. Two, they have the smarts to do it and want to make a lot of money. It's the first that makes a great doctor. What is the reason you want to go into medicine?"

Josh took a deep breath. "I keep seeing the men I was supposed to be leading getting killed in the paddies. There was nothing I could do to help. I was totally helpless. I don't want that to happen again."

Bruce looked across the table intently. "That's not enough. In the coming years, you will see each of the beatitudes come across your practice. What are you going to do? You will have choices you have to make. What are you going to do with those choices? You have decisions you must make before you start. Look at each of the beatitudes. All those people are going to come across your path. How are you going to deal with them?"

Josh looked at Bruce. "Look, bro, how am I supposed to deal with those people when I have all this junk going on inside my head? How on God's green earth do I deal with someone who is in mourning when I still am not over all those kids who were killed under my command?"

Bruce smiled. "Buddy, you have got work to do. You will find as you work to build other people up, as you work to help people who have their own issues, you will be helped as well. That's how God's economy works. The more you give, the more you get. You give love, you receive it back. You touch people who mourn, you are helped in your own mourning."

"Okay, bro. Let me see if I am getting this straight. God's economy is not about getting ahead of our brothers. It's about lifting our brother up. Is that correct?" Josh asked.

"I think you're starting to get it," Bruce replied.

"Bro, I have this strange feeling this is not limited to a person's occupation. This will take place in anything we do. Are we supposed to be looking for one of the 'blessed' individuals at all times?"

Bruce smiled as he said, "The cool thing about this whole thing is this. These blessed people don't always need anything from us except our support. For instance, we see a person who hungers and thirsts after righteousness. We should let them know we are behind them. We should be giving them encouragement for what they are doing. The same with peacemakers. These are the people who are sold out to Christ. These are people living their calling. We all need support from our fellow believers in all that Christ has called them to do. The question is this. Are we going to be that person who supports our fellow believers in what they are called to do or not?"

Josh leaned back in his seat. "So, what you're telling me is this. It's not about us. It's about what we do to touch others. It's about the support that we give people who are set on carrying out their mission in life. But what about the men who died in Nam? What about my not being able to help them? What about my feeling guilty about still being alive and there dead?"

Bruce got a tear in his eye. "It's like this. I don't have the answer to why some of those men died ahead of their time and some did not. I can't even tell you that they are all in heaven. But this, I can tell you—God is not done with you. You are still here because God the Father—through his Son, by his Spirit—is not done with you yet. He has much more for you to accomplish. I don't have all the answers, but the answers I do have, you will get from me. There is war because man is sinful. There is war because man wants to be in command of more people. There is war because men in high towers get to decide what young men will do. Some countries will not go to war unless they are attacked. There are countries who go to war to protect themselves from being attacked. There are countries who go to war to own another country. But it's not the young men fighting who decide to go to war. It's the men in the ivory towers who send them to war to die. Pilate condemned Christ to die on the cross. It was his soldier who drove the nails into his hands and feet. It was his soldiers who lifted the cross into place. It was man's sinfulness that completed the destruction of sin by nailing Christ to the cross. There is still a war going on today. That war is not one country taking land from another country for itself. It is for the hearts and minds of everyone on this earth. It's to save men from the ultimate destruction of hell. I don't have all the answers, but this, I do know. You are here not because our Father needs you to save men from dying but from dying and going to hell."

Josh put his face in his hands. He looked up and said, "I am here because God is not through with me. But it seems to me that the only choice we have is who are we going to serve? Is that correct?"

"It's like this. When man thinks he is doing things on his own, when he thinks that he is in control, that's when he is in the least control. You see, my friend, it's like this. When we are serving the Father, we are given things to do every day. Those things are to build up those we work or have some relationship with. That relationship may last a few minutes or hours or years. We are told to do something. We can choose to do it or not. But when a person thinks they are doing things on their own, when they think they are in control, that's when the enemy has them right where he wants them. When we are serving the living God through his Son, by his Spirit, that's when we will have total fulfillment. Remember, Jesus said in the gospels of Mark and Matthew, 'What good does it do to gain the world and lose one's soul?' Remember this. Our choice is who are we going to serve? This, I do know. The words I want to hear from my Father in heaven are these. "Well done, good and faithful servant." If I hear those words, everything he has had me do on this earth will have been worth it," Bruce said.

Josh took another sip of his coffee. "I see what you're saying. I can see it in my own life. Every day we have choices. Those choices are not about what we are doing but about who we will serve. Those choices are about being the best servants we can be for the one whom we are going to serve. Like the scripture says, as for me and my house, we will serve the Lord. But what do I do with all these flashbacks?"

"Let me make some phone calls. I have always believed that prayer works. Our Father in heaven hears our prayers and answers them. Jesus gives the peace that passes all understanding. It's that peace that I want you to start praying for. The next step is for you to see Jon Johnson. He is a Christian psychologist. He may be able to help. I know that he has dealt with a lot of guys in your situation. Let's take this one step at a time. I don't care what the enemy tries to do to derail you. God is greater. Jesus's peace is the peace that passes all understanding," Bruce said.

After a delicious lunch, Josh picked up the tab, and Bruce left a hefty tip for Jenna, the waitress. The two men left the Buckle and headed back to Josh's home.

The next two weeks, the two men would spend behind closed doors doing an in-depth study of the beatitudes. As Josh became better acquainted with them, he came to an understanding of them. As his understanding improved, he was able to get a picture in his mind of what the individuals who would come across his path would look like. The one thing he did understand was that he still had two years of residency left before he would go into practice, but those two years would pass quickly.

CHAPTER 3

The Beatitudes Begin

Blessed Are the Poor in Spirit

On July 19, 2025, Josh's alarm would sound. The trumpets would be blowing "Reveille" on his alarm clock. He popped up, as was his usual schedule.

He leaned over with a huge smile on his face and looked at his beautiful Sharon. "Babes today is the day. Today I start my residency. Today I will be able to finally start to treat people. Today I can start to be the Father's instrument to touch people. Today I am somebody."

"Wait a minute, bucko. Who has been feeding you that line about not being somebody? You have been praying with patients for your whole time in med school. You have led countless people to Christ as you went through both your grad and undergrad studies. Don't even give me that."

Josh chuckled. "You know what I mean. The title adds credibility to the whole process. Having 'Doctor' in front of the name sounds more official."

Sharon nodded. "Okay, I will give you that. Just don't let it go to your head. Remember, the scripture does say that pride comes before destruction."

Shaking his head, Josh gave a weak smile. "Okay, I hear you. Let me just go to work and see who God is going to touch through me today."

Two hours later, he walked into Memorial Hospital and took the elevator to the fifth floor.

He walked down the hall to speak with the head nurse, Janet Smith. "Ms. Smith, who should I call on first?"

Janet looked at Josh. "We have a Nancy Todd in 52. She is suffering with pancreatic cancer. She is mad at the world. Why don't you go see what you can do for her?"

Josh walked down the hall, gave a slight knock on the door, stuck his head in, and almost got it knocked off when a vase smashed against the door.

Josh jumped back. "What is going on here? Why the vase?"

He jumped inside the room and got ready to duck again. He looked at Nancy, an attractive lady, aged fifty-two.

"What did I ever do to you? Hold your fire. Let's talk," Josh said as he got ready to duck again. "You are making me feel like I am back in Nam, trying to duck the fire from the VC."

Nancy gave Josh a weak smile. "Dr. Henderson, I am sorry. I know I don't have much time left here. I just want to feel alive while I am still here. It's like I am lying here, waiting to check out. There is nothing I can do anymore to leave anyone anything that says I was here."

Just then, the words spoken by Bruce Johnson went through his mind. *Live the beatitudes. Be the person who brings the blessing.* At that moment, the words hit Josh like a ton of bricks. "Nancy, how can I be a blessing to you? What can I do so your life can have meaning? Let me ask you a few questions. Are you a Christian?"

The answer was immediate and angry. "Hell no! No way. I would never buy into that fairy tale. What has the so-called God ever done for me? I am here dying. I have no legacy. He has not shown his reality to me."

Josh looked directly at Nancy. "Nancy, I have seen a lot of crap in my life, but I have also seen some miraculous things happen. I do know this. The day he created us; he knew the day we would cease to exist on this earth. Our end is going one of two places. One will be amazing, the other, well, not so much. But the question we each have to answer is where do we want to go?"

Nancy looked at Josh with anger in her eyes. "I will go in the ground and rot."

Josh took her hand. "What if you're wrong? Why not simply ask Christ that if he is here, he will show you that he is real?"

"Just get out. Get out!"

Josh started to walk out.

"Stop. Please stop," Nancy begged.

Josh stopped short. "Nancy, what is it I can do for you?"

"Doctor, I don't want to die. I have wasted my life. I need more time. Please help me."

At that second, the words went through his mind. *Blessed are the poor in spirit, for theirs is the kingdom of heaven.*

"Doctor, I know where this is going to end up. I also know that I come to God having totally blown my life. How do I receive Jesus? How do I become a believer who can make a difference to those around me? I have so little time left. Can you help me?"

Josh knew he had to step up on this one. "Nancy, would you like to pray with me right now and receive Christ?"

"Yes," Nancy answered immediately.

Josh proceeded to lead Nancy in a prayer of repentance and acceptance of everything Jesus had to offer. They also prayed that Nancy would find her role in the Father's purpose, that her emptiness would be filled with the Father's abundance, and that her remaining days on this earth would be used to touch people in ways that would change people's lives forever.

The peace that came over Nancy at that point in time was an

amazing thing to behold. Instead of anger, there was peace. Her strength increased. When her doctor came in the next day, he was amazed. Nancy smiled at him and asked if she could go home for a while. She knew she would be coming back, but if she could get a few weeks at home, perhaps, just perhaps, she could do something that would leave some kind of legacy.

The doctor smiled. "Has Dr. Henderson been of help to you, Nancy?"

"More than you will ever know, Doctor. My life now has some meaning to it."

Dr. Ormsby looked at Josh. "Josh, could you or your bride be of service in this instance? Take her to her home. Make sure she is okay. Also, could you contact her family so there is someone there twenty- four hours a day?"

Josh picked up his phone and dialed Sharon. "Babes, I need your help. There is this lady, Nancy, with pancreatic cancer. The Father is doing some amazing things with her. She has the strength to go home. Can you help drive her home, help her contact family, and help get some things set up around her house?"

Sharon was smiling as she approached the hospital. She walked into Nancy's room and introduced herself. Nancy smiled and started getting ready to leave the hospital a few days earlier and thought she would be dying in a few days. As Sharon walked into Nancy's house with her, the handmade tapestry on the wall caught her attention.

"Who made these?" Sharon asked Nancy.

"I did," Nancy answered.

"They are totally beautiful. Do you realize how much these could sell for? Your talent is amazing." Sharon said, smiling. Sharon walked over to Nancy and put her hands on Nancy's shoulders. "Nancy, God the Father has given us all some sort of creativeness. To some, it's music. To some, it's writing. To some, it's the ability to create with our hands. To some, it's being able to fix cars. But we are all created in God's image."

Nancy smiled. "I know what I have to create. I need to create a tapestry using the head of Christ. When my times comes, I want that tapestry over my casket. I know this now. Christ has everything. I have nothing. I wish I would have realized that sooner. We as humans are bankrupt. We have nothing that we can bring. Anything we gain, any person that we can reach—it is not us. Any people reached by us are reached through us. Now I understand what the term 'filthy rags' is all about. Any good within us is as filthy rags. Rags that are used to change oil in a car. Once they are used, they are thrown out. That's what we think our good is. When we think we are great, that's when we are really nothing. When we realize we have and are nothing compared to our Father, that's when he can use us."

Nancy lived three months. In that time, she grew closer to the

Lord. She found herself with huge regrets about not having the time to accomplish anything for the kingdom of God, but she worked on her tapestry. She worked for two months at home and then took it to the hospital with her for her last stay there. The day after she finished the tapestry, she died. Her daughter had been able to make peace with her mom. After the funeral, Josh was able to hand her daughter the tapestry and, with a smile, blessed her.

CHAPTER 4

Blessed Are Those Who Mourn

Josh was sitting in his office. Sue, the nurse, brought in his next patient, Theresa McVeigh. She had been in a skiing accident and broke her arm. His first thought was that this would be easy. *A quick cast, and she's out the door.*

As she walked into his office, he noticed her striking beauty. Josh did a quick exam on her arm and sent her down for X-rays. When she returned, the nurse was carrying her purse for her. After Josh had set her arm, she pulled a picture out of her purse.

"Dr. Josh, this is a picture of my late husband, Chad. As you can see, you have your arm around him. I believe this was just before he was killed in that rice paddy you led them into."

Josh held the picture in his hand. He could not take his eyes off the picture. The guilt he felt, and the loss of friendship were crushing. He looked into the angry eyes of Theresa as she sat across from him. In her mind, she was wondering how much damage she could do to Josh with her cast if she hit him in the head. Tears starting to run down Josh's cheeks. He had to divert his eyes from Theresa's as he could not stand to even look at her. His shame was overwhelming him. He had led them into the paddy where so many of his men had been killed.

He looked at Theresa and could only say a few words. "I am so sorry. So, so sorry."

Theresa exploded. "Is that all you have to say? You're sorry? How on God's green earth can that be all you have to say? You're sorry. What kind of worthless piece of human refuge are you? All you have to say is you're sorry?"

"Theresa, I can see you still hurt a lot. I can't bring him back. That war hurt so many people. The only thing I can ask for is this. Please forgive me. I could use the platitude that I was just following orders. But in this instance, those words would do little good. Please forgive me—"

Theresa interrupted. "Don't you dare try to use that tactic on me. You have no idea the plans we had made before he was shipped off to your 'police action.' You see, it started when we were in high school. I was a cheerleader, and Chad was a basketball player. We dated all through our senior year. He had a basketball scholarship to Drake University. He wanted to be a coach. In the middle of his freshman year, he got drafted. He tried to get a college deferment but could not."

Josh sat in his office, listening to Theresa telling the story of their semester before Chad had to leave for boot camp.

*   *   *

It went like this. Chad walked out of the student affairs office. The look on his face was one of concern, anger, and confusion.

"Theresa, I am an engineering student. Sure, I play basketball, but they think the rest of my major is a ruse. They say they will only defer me to the end of this school year. July 15, I am off to boot camp. They are destroying our future. For what? Just so they can put another body on the ground in Nam. Why? Their objective is not to win the war. Their objective is to make money for the war industry. Why don't we let the North and South Vietnamese fight their own damn war? We have nothing to gain from it. I am a slave. They can draft me, and I must fight a war that should not be fought. What am I supposed to be doing?" Chad said.

Theresa walked over to Chad and kissed him. She then stepped back and said, "Sweetheart, you can't go into a war thinking about how wrong it is to fight the war. You must approach it with the idea that you are going to kill the other guy before he kills you. If you don't, you will come back in a body bag. I love you, Chad. I want to spend the rest of my life with you, but I can't do that if you're dead."

Chad nodded. "Sweetheart, the one thing I know is this. We have three months until the end of the school year. Because of my time in school, they are giving me a pay grade promotion right after boot camp. I think—"

Theresa interrupted. "Don't go there."

Chad, at this point, was dealing with a second disappointment in a short period. He took Theresa in his arms and just held her. He wanted to feel close. At that second, two people from InterVarsity Christian Fellowship walked up to them.

"Hey, guys. How ya doing?" John Smith asked them. "Aren't you the basketball star?"

"Not for long. I have been drafted. I went after a student deferment. I was denied."

"Look, we are having a mixer in the commons tonight. Why not join us? You just might like it," John said.

Chad looked at Theresa. "What do you think, babes?"

Theresa smiled. "It could be fun. It's going to have a bunch of students who are going to be totally moral."

Chad realized at that point, there would be something else he needed that they would have, something that all the basketball games he had won, all the great grades he would make could not fill. He was not sure what it would be, but he knew he had to find out.

———

Chad and Theresa walked into the student center. As they walked in, the greetings they received made them feel at home.

Chad looked into Theresa's eyes. "Babes, this should be really interesting."

They sat and listened and watched the students involved with IV get enthusiastic about the music. Then the young pastor who had volunteered preached a sermon on the saving blood of Christ. That night, both Theresa and Chad would make a serious commitment to Christ.

As Chad walked Theresa back to her dorm, he looked at her and said, "I feel like everything has changed. I feel different."

Theresa smiled as she said, "Chad, I feel like Christ is inside of me. I feel like a new person. I wonder if this is what it is like to be born again."

Chad looked at Theresa and said, "Look, last time, you stopped me. But I think that it is important that we consider getting married. Theresa, will you marry me before I go off to boot camp?"

The immediacy of the answer caught Chad off guard.

"Yes, yes, yes, yes, I will!"

Theresa jumped into Chad's arms, and they enjoyed a few moments where there was no one else in the world but them.

They looked at the young pastor who was leading IV that night. They asked them how quickly he could marry them. He told them they should talk to their parents first and see what they wanted to do.

The next weekend, they would drive to their hometowns. First, they would go to Theresa's, and Chad would ask her father for her hand in marriage. Then they would drive to Chad's and ask for his parents' blessings. Both sets of parents wanted a family wedding with a reception for their friends afterward.

The plans were made. The celebration was planned. Everyone was excited. The party was one for the ages. They were married on the Fourth of July. They had one week to honeymoon, and Chad was gone to boot camp.

*   *   *

Theresa looked at Josh. "Doc, I know I can't blame you for what happened to Chad. But it stinks. It really stinks. Our son Chad is now ten. He will never know his real dad. I have married again. It's not the same. Oh, don't get me wrong. I love Matt. He is a great man, loves Chad, but it's not the same."

Josh looked at Theresa and said, "Need a hug?"

"Yes, please," she answered, and a hug was given.

"May I pray for you?" Josh whispered to her as he hugged her.

Theresa stepped back. "Dr. Josh, I am sorry. I am not really into that. How could a loving God allow such a terrible thing to happen? How?"

"Theresa, I am going to tell you the same thing my nurse from

Nam told me. She is now my beloved bride. It's a nasty thing called sin. All one must do is go back to Adam and Eve. The choice they made to rebel against the Father would separate them from God forever—that is, until God sent his only Son to die for their sins. The only problem is this. Man is still sinning today. Think of the price that is going to be paid by the evil that was delivered on the young from both sides for having a war for the sole purpose of making money. A lot of brave soldiers died for nothing. Don't get me wrong. The ones who returned, those soldiers who came home—they deserve a hero's welcome. It's the politicians who deserve the wrath of the people who lost sons, brothers, and fathers. God is not to blame for their sin. Unless they repent—I mean totally, honestly, in sack cloth and ashes—there won't be much mercy for them. The blood of a lot of young men will be on their heads."

Theresa got a look of discernment on her face. "I think I am starting to get this. We had a government that was being paid by the arms industry to not end a war that was getting a lot of good young men killed. That government sent both my husband and you to fight a war that did not need to be fought. We were doing what Japan did to us in World War II. They attacked us without reason. They sought to disable our Pacific fleet so they could eventually take us over. Only in Vietnam, we were more intent in using weapons to make money for the guys who made the weapons. The arms people were willing to let thousands of innocent kids die on both sides so they could make money?"

"You got it," Josh answered.

Theresa started to get red in the face. "That just makes me angrier. How in God's green earth do we make sure this never happens again?"

Josh looked at Theresa. "Get active. Make your voice heard. If we sit back, like what happened when we got into this 'conflict' in the first place, it will happen again. I have no problem taking another country down that wants to make the mistake of taking us on. But getting involved with getting a bunch of people killed for no reason? That is lunacy."

"You know, Doc, knowing all the reasons is all well and good. But that still does not help me feeling I have been robbed. I feel like the best person I have ever had in my life was stolen from me. What can I do about that?"

"Theresa, I can't tell you how to mourn your loss. The same way you can't tell me how do deal with seeing all those bright young men die in that rice paddy. Or how I deal with the fact that that stupid war cost me half my leg. What I have found that helps is asking God the Father through the Son, by His Spirit, one question in the morning. 'Who are you going to touch through me today?' I have found that by being used by the Father to help other people gives me a sense of fulfilment, that maybe, just maybe, it was something worthwhile in some way."

Theresa got a slight smile on her face. "Now you can pray for me. Now I am ready to let God touch me and use me."

Josh prayed. "Father, I lift Theresa to you. I know you have built us all as individuals. I just pray that somehow, in some way, you will be able to touch her by touching others through her. I pray her son Chad will grow to be a man after your own heart. He will be a man who will work to build your kingdom. In Jesus's name. Amen."

Theresa would be Josh's last patient of the day. He drove home and walked into the house.

Sharon was there to meet him. "How was your day, babes?"

Josh plopped down on a chair next to the table. "Sweetheart, it was interesting. This lady came in with a physical problem. Her physical problems seemed to disappear when she found out just who I was. You see, her late husband was one of the guys under my command when we got caught in a rice paddy. She is going through the mourning process still. As I bet for every woman who was involved with the guys whom I commanded. We talked for a couple of hours about the whole situation. In the end, I was able to pray with her and hopefully help her with her mourning. Babes, it's such a long process."

"Josh, do you remember what Bruce told you? You are going to see each of the blessed people from the beatitudes come across your path. You are supposed to lift them by being that blessing. You are supposed to lift them by letting the Father—through his Son, by his Spirit—lead you in ways that will make you a blessing to them. You will be blessed in being a blessing to them."

Josh looked at his beautiful bride. "Babes, it's great to be used, to be a blessing. But it is also totally exhausting. I have come to this conclusion. Our Father—through his Son, by his Spirit—is going to bring people across my path whom he can use me to touch. It was not by accident that Theresa came into our office to get her arm taken care of. As a matter of fact, I think the Holy Spirit may have decided to use the 'accident' she had to help her deal with the mourning she is in.

"It seems to me that when a person is in mourning, there is always that underlying grief in their system that can guide their choices in how any given situation is dealt with. Every day I wake up and look out the window. I see my men getting mowed down in the rice paddy. Every day I feel the anger well up in me over our government getting involved in something that was pointless except to make money. All they accomplished was getting a bunch of men killed. I have come to the realization that the only way I can end this mourning is to be able to forgive what has been done to my men and myself. That is where Theresa was at as well.

"We all mourn at some point. Jesus said, 'Blessed are those who mourn, for they shall be comforted.' I think our Father is going to use each of us to be the blessings. In every instance, we must be praying and asking how to handle each situation."

CHAPTER 5

Blessed Are the Meek (Carl)

A few months went by. Josh's patients had been everything, from the flu to initial cancer screenings. On Monday, June 17, Carl Adams walked through his door. He stood six feet and six inches tall. His voice sounded like a bass drum; it was so deep. His arms were huge. When he shook Josh's hand, Josh felt like he would break it. His grip was so strong.

"Mr. Adams, I see you have a rash on your arm. What have you been in contact with?" Josh asked.

"Dr. Josh, I work down at the animal shelter. I am in contact with cats and dogs and gerbils and every other kind of pet you can imagine. I have no idea what could have caused this rash."

"Carl, I suspect that it is not one of the animals you are dealing with but some sort of cleaning agent that you come in contact with. What are your responsibilities at the shelter?"

"Mostly keeping the cages clean and doing any heavy lifting they need."

At that second, they heard a scream coming from the waiting room. They both got up to run out and see what was going on. They would find a man with a gun, pointing it at the pharmacist, demanding drugs.

Josh's first thought was to take the guy out, but Carl walked up behind the guy quietly, grabbed his wrist, and quietly said, "Mister, if I were you, I would set the gun on the counter. It will not go as bad for you."

The man realized that unless he set the gun down, he would get his arm broken. While Carl held his arm, he slowly moved his hand to the counter to set the gun on the counter. He then set the gun on the counter, and Carl walked him over to one of the chairs in the waiting room, where they waited for the police to arrive.

After the man was taken into custody, Josh and Carl went back into the exam room. At this point Josh was starting to understand what "blessed are the meek" meant.

"Carl, you controlled that situation quite professionally. What is your training background?"

"Aw, shucks, it was no big deal. Just plain old common sense. I looked at the guy. He was desperate. He thought he really needed a fix. That was not going to do him any good at all. I think he was actually hoping to get caught. He will have to spend some jail time, but he will be without the demons of the drugs that haunt him."

"I have to ask you this question, Carl. What if he would have pulled the gun away and shot you?"

The mountain of a man smiled at Josh. "Dr. J, first, I trust that God himself placed me here for such a time as this. Second, if he would have moved his hand toward me with the gun in it, I would have broken his arm. Probably would have been a compound fracture. I wasn't too worried. Besides, God is my protector. I had nothing to worry about."

Josh shook his head. "Carl, I see something in you. I see a quiet strength that can deal with people on a level I see in very few people. Have you given any thought to another form of work, maybe something having more people contact?"

"Dr. J, I have plenty of people contact in what I am doing now. For instance, I was working with the 'truck' going out to pick up a stray dog. We found the dog, but there was this little girl who was petting the dog we came to pick up. We had no information on the dog. We did not know if it could be rabid or sick with something. All we knew was that we had to pick it up. We walked up to the dog. We were about to put the collar on it, and the little girl started crying. She wanted to keep the dog. You see, this little girl was homeless herself.

"Dr. J, my wife is a saint. I called her up and asked her if I could bring the little girl home. She said no. I was devastated. Then she said I had to call the police and child protective services, which I did. The next thing that happened was the police came, as did a social worker. I was to find out the little girl's name was Jayne. They asked her where her mommy lived. She told them her mommy had been with a bunch of men doing drugs and died. The police asked her what her mommy's name was. She told them. They radioed the station and confirmed that she was telling the truth. Let me say this. We now have the dog living in our home, and our daughter's name is Jayne."

"Dr. J, every animal has a story. It's impossible to find the story on every animal. I really feel that I have been placed in this position to be able to help people. I do that by helping animals. Most of the people I help are one-time acquaintances. But there are times when lifelong friendships have developed. In the case of Jayne, we would never have met if God—through his Son Jesus, by his Holy Spirit—had not 'arranged' for this stray pug to be out on the street. This little girl needed love. She needed someone to care. The pug gave her that. Yet in the long run, we knew it would not be enough. My wife Janet and I realized that we were placed in her life and she in ours for the purpose of doing something positive in God's plan on this earth. All we must do is what he is leading us to do. For now, anyway, for me, that means taking care of the animals who take care of people."

Josh looked directly into Carl's eyes. "Carl, you're six feet and six inches tall. You weigh 275 pounds. I could see you doing a lot more strenuous work than catching stray animals. How satisfying do you really find this work?"

"Look, Dr. J, it's like this. I don't care about fame or fortune. I care about people. I have found the best way to reach people is with a cute puppy or kitten. I see hearts change in a second. I see dads who are ticked that they are even looking at animals have their hearts melted. God has put it in pets to be that instrument to soften people."

At that second, Josh's cell rang. It was Sharon.

"Hey, babes. What's up? I am with a patient."

"Josh, I hesitated to call. I kind of figured you would be with a patient. Is there any way we can get a pug?" Sharon asked.

"A pug?" was the quick response.

Carl smiled. "We just got one in. Have your bride there in an hour. I will see her there." Smiling, he stood up.

Josh looked up at this mountain of a man and smiled. "Carl, may I ask you a personal question?"

"Sure. What's on your mind?"

"Carl, what is your faith situation?"

"Doc, what do you mean?"

Josh could see in this instance he had to be direct and to the point. "Are you a Christian?"

"Can't you tell?" Carl answered.

Josh smiled. "Yes, it pretty obvious."

Carl chuckled. "Jesus leads every step I take. I feel like God the Father—through the Son, by the Spirit—leads me daily. He brings the animals across our path that will touch the hearts of those who need to be touched. Think of it this way. Have you ever felt angry or even really sad? At that second, your cat jumps up on your lap. You start petting it. It purrs. Suddenly, you feel the tension go out of you. You feel a calmness come over you. That's God the Father using his pet cat to touch you.

"You see, my friend, it's not about us or how great we think we are. It's about what our Father—through his Son, by his Spirit—does through us. We cannot—we must not—take credit for what the Father does through us. There is no greater thrill in this world than being used by the creator of the universe to touch someone. Remember this. Jesus, when he walked out of the grave, was and is bringing glory to his Father because of it. Remember, you will see some amazing things happen because of what the Father—through the Son, by the Spirit—is going to do through you. You have been given a platform. Mine is bringing animals to those who are really hurting. Yours is working as a doc, to see people in physical pain brought back to health. Just remember this. Physical health is temporary. Spiritual health will last forever."

Josh looked at Carl. "Bro, you have taught me a lot today. My first thought when I saw you walk in was 'This guy is big, probably not real bright.' Man, I was wrong in half of that! You are big. But you are also extremely bright. You know what the Holy Spirit has placed you in this life to do and why. I am seeing more and more clearly why I have been placed here. I am also seeing what a friend of mine meant when he told me to live the beatitudes. I am starting to see what the characteristics of each one look like."

Carl stepped back as he put his shirt back on and as he got ready to leave. "Dr. J, you have been given an amazing platform. But would you tell me something? What beatitude do I fit?"

Josh smiled. "Carl, you're meek. You have a strength that is quiet. You use the power you have been given in such a quiet way. You use it to touch people with the pets you give them. You don't make a big deal about it. You just do what you have been created to do every day without fanfare."

Carl smiled with a huge toothy smile. "We both have jobs to do. We are put here with the same purpose in mind. That is to take a role in our Father's purpose. His purpose is to touch his kids in a way that will change their lives forever."

With that, he got up. His massive frame made Josh feel like a midget. Carl walked over to Josh and gave him a huge hug. He smiled and walked out of his office.

CHAPTER 6

Blessed Are the Peacemakers

After a couple of weeks, Josh was transferred to the ER.

He walked and asked the head doctor, "Anyone to see right now?"

Dr. Smith looked over at Josh. "Right now, we have a policeman headed here in an ambulance. He has taken a bullet in the spine. He can still move his lower extremities. We must be extremely careful. One false move, and he is paralyzed from the waist down."

At that moment, they heard the ambulance come up to the garage door of the ER. The crew were very careful to get Officer Haggy into the ER without any more injuries to his spine. Dr. Smith ordered a CT scan on his back. The caution used in moving him was extreme. They were to find out that the bullet was lodged between the sixth and seventh vertebrae.

Dr. Smith looked over at Josh and asked if he would like to scrub in. Josh nodded and proceeded to assist with a very delicate surgery. After the surgery, Officer Haggy was taken back to his room. As he awoke, Josh was beside his bed.

He looked at Josh and smiled. "Officer Haggy."

"Jim," the officer stated.

"Jim, do you remember what happened?" Josh asked.

"Doctor, it was like this. I was walking the beat and heard a scream. It was down an alley. I saw this guy trying to take a baby from its mother. I pulled my gun and order him to halt. He stopped cold. Holding the child in one arm, he pointed his gun at me. I raised mine. He threatened to shoot the baby. I quickly aimed my gun at his head and pulled the trigger. He fell, and the baby landed on top of him, but I did not see his buddy coming up behind me. He put a bullet in my back. I fell to the ground, looked behind me, and dropped him as well. The mom called 911. The next thing I remember is being in the ambulance."

Immediately, in his mind's eye, Josh could see his men dying in the rice paddy. He shook his head to bring himself back to reality. He looked at Jim and realized this was another "beatitude."

"Jim, can you wiggle your toes?" Josh asked.

Josh watched as Jim wiggled his toes.

"We are going to be very gentle with you over the next few

---

weeks. I hope you like hospital food. You're going to be eating it for a while."

Nurse Johnson stuck her head through Jim's door. "Mr. Haggy, you have a visitor. May I show her in?"

"Please do" was the quick reply from Jim.

Gwen was shown into Jim's room. "Officer Haggy, you saved my daughter Samantha. How can I thank you?" she asked.

"Just raise her to be a godly woman. May I hold the little princess?" he asked.

As Gwen handed the baby to Jim, she said, "Samantha, this is Officer Haggy. He saved your life. Your daddy was instrumental in giving you your life. This man is the reason you got to keep it."

Jim sat holding the precious little girl. He wiggled his toes again. He looked to heaven and prayed. "Father, I give this little girl to you. I ask that you touch her, you keep her safe, and you give her a heart for you and your kingdom that cannot be turned away from your purpose. Father, I pray that you will use her to bring many people into your kingdom. Father, use Gwen to touch people in ways that will change their lives forever. Protect her from the enemy. He tried to take her out once. Keep her safe, please. In Jesus's name. Amen."

Gwen was crying. She knew that the prayer Jim had just prayed was heard by the Father in heaven. She understood that her little girl had been saved for a reason, and that reason was huge.

*　　*　　*

Eighteen years later, Officer Haggy would be the honored guest at the very first concert of Sophie Larson. Her sweet, soft voice had captured the attention of one of the largest Christian recording studios in the country. He would walk into the arena and would be taken backstage to meet with Gwen and Sophie. He knocked on their dressing room door, stated his name, was ushered in, and was hit with a hug that few could even imagine.

"Officer Haggy, I am here because of you. If you had not done what you did that day, I would not be here," Sophie stated with tears in her eyes.

Jim looked at Sophie. "Sweetheart, you are here because God our Father—through his Son Jesus, by his Holy Spirit—put me in the right place at the right time. I was doing what I was created to do so you could be here tonight to do what you were created to do. But that was a great hug," he said, smiling.

*　　*　　*

Josh looked at Jim, having just seen the vision of what was to come in his life. He realized exactly what Bruce Johnson had been talking about that day a few years back over coffee. The beatitudes that Christ had given his followers on the mount was a conversation about real people. They represented life experiences. Some of the people were people who would make life better for others living out other beatitudes. Josh smiled as he thought about

Christ bringing across his path other people living out their beatitudes. He smiled at the thought of just how much life was about living the beatitudes.

The next day, he walked into Jim's room. Jim was sitting up in bed.

"Doc, I wonder what little Gwen is going to do with her life."

Josh had seen what God had in mind for that little girl. He knew the experience this young officer would have in about eighteen years.

All he could say was "I can only imagine."

In the next few weeks, Jim would get more feeling in his legs. He would walk out of the hospital. He would walk out on a beautiful sunny day. He would be blessed in his work as a peacemaker for the next twenty-five years.

CHAPTER 7

Blessed Are Those Persecuted for Righteousness' Sake

Josh walked through the door, fell on the couch, and just rested.

Sharon walked up to where he lay, kissed him on the forehead, and asked, "Babes, tough day?"

"Not really that tough, but there was a lot going on. You spoke with Carl. You better get down tomorrow and get your pup. But Officer Jim was the tough one. He had a visitor while in my office."

"What? How? You're not supposed to be interrupted while you're in an exam."

"I know, but when she saw Jim go in, she had to see him. She was there for a well-baby checkup. Jim had just saved the baby.

She came in and told the story. What Jim did was amazing."

"Care to share it with me?" Sharon asked.

For the next thirty minutes, Josh would share how Jim was able to save little baby Sophie.

Then he looked at his beautiful bride and asked, "Babes, would it be all right if I took off for a bit and went on a few miles' run?"

Sharon smiled. "Only if I can go with you."

"Sure, babes. Let's go."

Both changed into their sweats and hit the street. They had been running for a mile when they came along a father and daughter having an argument with a public-school superintendent. They could see the father staying calm, while the superintendent yelled at him. They could hear the father from where they were standing.

"How can you have my daughter get an F on a paper that deserves much better than that? You know as well as I do, she gave totally reasoned-out arguments on why the 'theory' of evolution is predicated on a false premise. You have said yourself the paper was well thought out."

The anger in the super was evident. "And tell me, sir—what makes you such an authority on the arguments of evolution versus creation?"

"I am Dr. Sam Johnson. I have authored ten books on

creation. My doctorate is in astrophysics. Are you familiar with the big bang theory? Well, let me tell you something. I understand what happened at the big bang. That was the point when there was nothing. Everything was in the dark. There was no light. There was nothing that produced light. Then God the Father spoke. I can only imagine the sound when all heaven broke loose. When millions of suns burst their energy into light in a second," the dad said with a smile on his face.

The superintendent became angrier. "You know we can't teach that here. That brings 'religion' into it. We can't do that."

The father had a rage building inside of him because they were feeding his daughter lies. "How can you teach this stuff when you know it's a pack of lies? How can you feed lies to innocent kids?"

"Separation of church and state," the super said.

"I will see you in court," the dad responded.

Josh looked at his bride. "Let's go see if we can help."

Sharon got a worried look on her face. "Are you sure we should do that?"

"Absolutely. We are all in this thing together."

They walked over to the arguing folks.

"Hello, I am Dr. Joshua Henderson. This is my wife, Sharon. Mr. Superintendent, why are you trying to stifle this young lady and her First Amendment rights? She is not forcing anyone to believe her arguments. She is putting them forth in a well-thought-out format. I have not read it, but from what I heard you folks talking about, it was a well-thought-out paper. I think, sir, you are looking at a lawsuit that you can't win. It may end up in the Supreme Court, but you will lose. I have heard your looking to pass a bond issue to be used for an addition to your building. How's it going to look when it hits the paper that you are willing to spend millions on a lawsuit that only wants to take away a young lady's First Amendment rights?"

The super turned and walked away. He could be seen waving his hands in the air as he walked around the parking lot. After ten minutes, he turned and walked back to the four people standing in the parking lot who had just given him a dose of reality.

"All right, you win. I will instruct the teacher to examine the paper the same way he would any other paper. It will be evaluated on its merit."

Josh looked at the super. "That is a wise choice. This political correctness has to stop." He then turned to the dad and his daughter. "Here's my card." He turned it and wrote his cell number on the back. "Give me a call and let me know how this turns out."

Dr. Sam looked at Josh. "You know I will. We will let you know exactly what happens."

Three days later, Dr. Sam's daughter called Josh on his cell phone.

"Dr. Josh, I got an A on the paper. Thank you so much for the help last Thursday. Without you, I would be sitting with an F. That would have really messed up my getting into college."

"Young lady, what have you learned from all this?" Josh asked.

"Dr. Josh, it's like this. No matter what, we have to stand for that which God the Father—through his Son, by his Spirit—shows us to be right. We cannot compromise on that which is right. We must stand for the right no matter what the cost. We cannot compromise."

Josh smiled to himself. "Young lady, you got it. There are times when we are persecuted for that which is right and just. We must remember that we cannot compromise on that which is right. But we will be blessed for making the stand."

*   *   *

The Journey Continues

The following day was Sunday. Sharon and Josh woke up early to make the 8:00 a.m. service.

As they drove up to the church, Sharon had a sheepish smile on her face. "Well, sweetie, last week, you experienced what living the beatitudes really means. What are you going to do with it?"

The look in Josh's face was one of saying, "I don't know. I feel I understand more of what Jesus is all about. As we see the beatitudes, we must understand one thing. All the beatitudes start the same way. 'Blessed are.' There is only one place that blessings come from. That is the Father, through the Son, by the Spirit. In many cases, however, we are the tools of the blessings."

Sharon smiled. "In other words, what Jesus was saying was we need to be aware of the people in every category. By being aware, we can then be put in a place to bless people in every situation. Some will be good. Blessing comes by encouragement. In other situations, blessing comes through compassion."

Josh walked across the room. "Remember a while back. We were active in the Methodist church of Lakeside. The had an energetic young pastor who was able to bring people to Christ. The problem was as the young believers came to Christ; they left the older folks behind. This caused a major church to split, which did not have to happen. There was a zeal for the Father through the Son, by the Spirit. But that zeal did not contain compassion. These longtime members were in mourning over the loss of the church, and the young folks at the heart of the revival did not seem to care. People mourn over several things. This loss was crucial to them. Many of the people had a deep faith in Christ. They expressed it in a way that fit them. That whole thing was turned upside down. They lost their ability to worship the Lord in the way they best understood. The younger crowd just did not seem to understand or care."

Sharon, as she listened, was almost in tears. "What happened?"

"Well, hon, the church split. A new church was started, the young pastor would lead it, and the Methodist church would suffer and die a slow death. That church died a death that, in my humble opinion, did not have to happen. Those people were in mourning, and the young folks, in their enthusiasm, did not care."

They finished dressing quickly, walked out the door, and headed for the church they were attending. As they walked in, the first person they would see was Josh's chief surgeon.

"Josh, how are you this fine day?" Dr. Peterson stated with a jovial tone.

Josh smiled. "Dr. Peterson, how are you? I did not know you attended this church."

Dr. Dave Peterson looked at Josh as he answered, "Josh, I am the guest speaker today."

Josh got a quizzical look on his face. "What is your topic this morning?"

"I am speaking on one of the beatitudes. 'Blessed are the meek.' It appears to me that people do not understand what 'meek' really means."

Josh, knowing the answer, still had to ask the question. "Doc, 'meek' is speaking about quiet strength, is it not?"

The chuckle from Dr. Peterson was evident. "Josh, how did you come up with that? Your definition is spot on."

"Dr. Peterson, it's like this. A few years ago, I had a man in my office. He was huge. He was able to take a very tense situation and saved lives because of his quiet strength. He demonstrated meekness."

"Would you expound on that?" Dr. Peterson asked Josh.

Josh smiled. "How much time do you have?"

The doctor knew he had something he could use. He would spend a couple of hours after church listening intently to Josh and how meekness in the economy of heaven really worked. It became clear to Josh through the conversation he was having with Doc Peterson that God's economy was far different than man's.

Josh's mind went back, once again, to the rice paddy. He could see his men getting cut down by the VC. He could hear his men screaming in pain. He could see the blood.

Then Dr. Peterson's voice broke in. "Josh, what's going on?"

"Doc, it's like this. When God the Father—through his Son, by his Spirit—led me through living the beatitudes, I thought those visions were beaten and gone. Evidently, they were not. Doc, what can I do? How can I make these visions go away?"

Dr. Peterson looked at Josh, shaking his head slightly. "Josh, I don't know that you will ever be able to make those visions go away. The only thing I can say is to use them to defeat the enemy."

"Defeat the enemy? How can I use these flashbacks to defeat the enemy?"

"How many men were killed that day?" the doc asked.

"About a hundred," Josh answered.

"I imagine they all had families."

Josh started to have a tear in his eye. "I'm sure," he answered.

"You need to start touching them in prayer every time you have one of those visions. You need to find the name of every man who died that day. When you do, put it on the wall of your office. I would also pray that the Father would bring across your path family members of each of the fallen for you to have contact with," the doc responded.

"Why would I want to do that?" Josh asked. "I mean the personal contact with their families?"

"Josh, people need closure. Did not Jesus say, 'Blessed are those who mourn'? Jesus has compassion for those folks. They need closure." Josh looked at the doc as he walked across the room. "I get it. My mind goes back to a young lady whom I saw in my medical office. She knew I was her husband's officer in that paddy. She about took my head off. We were able to pray together. She was able to forgive me for my part in her husband's death. But man, I am not in a hurry to go through that a hundred times more."

Doc Peterson looked at Josh as a father would his son. "Josh, here's what I would suggest you do. When you get those flashbacks, start praying for all those families. When you do that, our Father in heaven— through his Son, by his Spirit—will start bringing people across your path whom only you can touch. When that happens, the Spirit himself will guide you as to how to touch the people he brings across your path. It may be one person. It may be a hundred. The only thing you must do is be that person whom God has created you to be and be used."

With that, Josh did not say a word. He merely nodded.

*   *   *

Life Takes a Turn

It only took a few days. Josh and Sharon were sitting on a park bench, enjoying a Sunday after church. They saw an old car drive by. The backfire from the engine was tremendous. Josh found himself back in the rice paddies again. He shook his head and grabbed Sharon's hand, and they started praying for all the families of all the men who had died that day in the mud of Vietnam.

As they started to leave the park, they saw a woman walking with her ten-year-old son. They nodded to one another, and she then stopped cold.

"You're him!" she yelled as they walked along.

"I'm who?" Josh responded.

"You're Lieutenant Josh. You're the reason I am a widow and young Sam has no father!" the woman yelled. "We had been on our honeymoon. Then he had to leave. He never even found out about the son I was carrying. I got pregnant on our honeymoon. He never knew about his son," she said in tears.

Sharon looked at Josh. "Josh, there must be something we can do to help."

"Ma'am, I cannot bring your husband back. But let me ask this question. What can we do to help you, and what is the name of your son?"

The woman started to have tears running down her face. "I

named him after his father. His name is Jon."

Josh then asked, "And may I ask your name?"

"I am Sarah," she responded.

"Sarah, could I walk over to that bench and just have a talk with Jon? I would like to get to know the young lad a bit."

Sarah looked at the proximity of the benches to their present location. She looked up to heaven as if to pray, Father, what do I do? "Go ahead," Sarah answered.

Josh and Jon then proceeded to walk over to the park bench.

"Jon, what do you like to do?" Josh asked.

Jon got a big smile on his face. "I like football and love to paint."

"What do you like to paint?" Josh asked the lad.

"I love to paint animals in the wild. Did you know some of the most vicious animals are the most loving to their own cubs? Mom tells me that God the Father has instilled in each of us a love for his kids that is a copy of the love he has for us. I have question for you. You were my dad's commanding officer, right?"

"That's correct, Jon."

"Did you know my dad well?"

"To be honest, I did not," Josh answered.

"How will I know that my dad is proud of the man I will be in a few years?" Jon asked.

"You do things that would make God proud of you. The one

thing from the brief encounter I had with your dad was this. He loved the Lord. You live your life in such a way as to make God the Father, through his Son Jesus, proud of you, and your dad will be proud of you."

Jon then smiled from ear to ear. The joy that the young man was feeling was something to behold. "I can do that. I will do that," he said with total confidence. "Will you help me?" he asked.

Josh smiled. "Here's my card. Call me anytime. I would be honored to help you in any way that I can."

As they walked back to his mom, Sarah watched her smiling son as he became more and more excited about the time and the prospect of more time, he would spend with Josh. Jon walked with a new confidence that his life would become something great because of what God the Father had started to put together in his life.

As they walked to Sharon and Sarah, Sarah smiled. "Jon, you look really happy. What did you two talk about over there?"

"How I know my dad will be proud of the man I become," he replied.

"And how is that?"

"Well, Mom, it's like this. If I do things that I know will make God proud of me, then I know Dad will be proud of me cause he is with God. And I asked Dr. Josh to help me. He gave me his card and told me I could call him anytime."

Sarah looked at Josh. Once again, the tears started to fall. "I hated you. I hated that you led your men into that ambush in the rice paddy. I hated that you left our son without a father. I hate that the United States government let so many young men die for no reason. Then you do this for our son. You give him the very words he needed to hear to keep on going now that his father is not with us anymore. I can't hate you. I want to, but I can't. What is God doing here?"

At that point, Sharon walked over and took Sarah's hands into hers. "Sarah, Josh did not want to take those men into that rice paddy. He was doing what he was ordered to do. God is doing some things inside of him as well as the people God the Father—through his Son Jesus, by his Holy Spirit—brings across his path. Your son does not have a father on this earth. He will bring strong men across his path who can help guide him through his life."

Sarah was crying uncontrollably. "Why does God love Jon so much?"

Sharon put her arm around her. "Sarah, he does not love Jon any more than anyone else. He wants us all to be the best we can be. He had his only begotten Son Jesus die and walk out of the grave so we can all be set free from the law of sin and death. He will see his dad when he crosses from the finite to the infinite. And if I were a betting woman, I would be willing to bet that his dad will be immensely proud of him."

Sarah had tears running down her eyes. "May I hug you?" she asked.

Sharon smiled as she opened her arms wide and gave Sarah a huge hug. They cried in each other's arms.

Josh stood there, looking at the two ladies holding each other. He looked to heaven and prayed. *Father, when will all the senseless killing stop? When will there be war no more?*

Micah 4:3 came to mind. "They will beat their swords into plough shares. There will be no more war." He smiled at the possibility. Then Matthew 24:6 hit him like a ton of bricks. "There shall be wars and rumors of war, but the end is not yet."

Josh looked to heaven. *I get it, Father. As long as man is inclined to sin, as long as one group of people wants to conquer another, there will be wars. Each country needs to protect themselves from the others. I get it.*

At that point, Jon asked him, "Why are there wars? Why do people want to kill each other just to take control of the other's country?"

Josh shook his head. "It's called sin. Let's take the United States. We got into the Vietnam War to stop communism. At least, that's what they told the people. Communism in and of itself, in my opinion, is an evil thing. The problem was this. We were not in it to win it. I can see so much evil in the way that war was conducted, it's not funny a bit. The people of this country went along, for a while, with the idea of stopping communism. But the arms producers, the plane builders, etc. did not want the war to stop. They were willing to let a lot of good men die so they could make money. It did not affect them. The almighty dollar is what they were really interested in. It was not their family that was losing loved ones for no reason."

Jon got a quizzical look on his face. "Mr. Josh, are there any wars that are justified?"

Josh thought for a moment. "Yes. Let's look back at history. December 7, 1941. The Japanese attacked our naval base at Pearl Harbor. That brought us into a war to stop evil. The Germans were gassing the Jewish people. Japan was conquering Asia. They knew that we could stop them with our navy. So, they tried to sink it. Our aircraft carriers were not at Pearl when they attacked. They killed over two thousand of our men. Yamamoto, the commander of the Japanese, made a statement that would ring true. 'I fear we have woken a sleeping giant.' Yes, Jon. Some wars are justified."

"But what about Vietnam?" Jon asked. "Was that a justified war?"

Josh got a look on his face of concern. "In my opinion, no, it was not. The United States had no real interest in the country's politics. They were no threat to the United States."

Jon looked at Josh with tears coming down his face. "So, you're telling me my dad died for nothing?"

Josh thought, *I blew that one. Help me, Lord. Give me words for this young boy.* "Not at all. Your dad died for his country. You see, at the time, there was a mindset that if Vietnam fell, all the other countries in the region would become communist as well. But to be honest, your dad died saving twenty other men in the platoon. He died giving his life for the other men over there."

"So, my dad was a hero then?"

"Absolutely. He died so other men could live."

Jon got a huge smile on his face. "Dr. Josh, would you ever reenlist in the service?"

"Jon, that's an interesting question. Would I be willing to fight to protect the freedoms we have in this country? Absolutely, I would. We have so many freedoms that other countries do not have. But would I be willing to become a soldier again? I would need to spend a lot of time in prayer to see if that was something that God our Father—through his Son Jesus, by His Holy Spirit— wanted me to do. If I was convinced that is what he wanted me to do, in a second."

Jon began to smile and cry at the same time. "Dr. Josh, I am so proud of my dad, but I really miss him. I never got to meet him. I hurt, yet I am proud, and I don't know what to do about that."

Josh put his arm around Jon's shoulder. "Son, it's like this. God will be there. He will hold you when you need it. You will almost be able to feel his arm around you. But if you ever need someone to talk to, call me. If I am with a patient, I will call you back. I promise."

Jon smiled at Josh as they got up and walked back to his mom. He wiped his tears as he walked up to her and gave her a huge hug. "I love you, Mom. Can we go home? I need to write Dad a letter."

Sarah smiled and put her arm around Jon. "What are you going to say?" she asked.

"Mom, it's between me and Dad," Jon said, still with moistness in his eyes.

Sarah looked at Josh and Sharon. "Thank you so much for what you have done today. I don't know how to thank you."

All Josh and Sharon did was smile and say, "It was a blessing to be able to help. We will be praying for you."

With that, Sarah and Jon left the park.

Josh took Sharon's hand. "Babes, when Bruce and I had lunch and he told me I had to live the beatitudes, I had no idea what he meant. Know I am starting to understand. It's not just in my office. It's also in parks, at church, and everywhere else I might be. I know there are going to be celebrations that go along with these. That, I am looking forward to."

*   *   *

The Hippie

Two days later, Josh woke up, dressed, and got ready to go to his office. He was now in a full practice of his own. Living only three blocks from his office, he walked most days. This day would prove to be different from the others. As he walked down the street, an old gentleman came from an alley and confronted him.

"You are one of those baby killers. You killed innocent people in Nam. How can you live with yourself?"

Josh felt the spark. He knew this "old" hippie was trying to make trouble forty years after the end of the "war." Josh nodded and attempted to just walk by.

The man jumped directly into Josh's path. "Answer me, baby killer. How can you live with yourself?"

Josh handed the man his business card. "If you really want to have a conversation about this, come to my office, give this to my receptionist, and she will set an appointment for you to come and talk to me about it. What you're trying to do here is start something that does not need to be started. I have patients to see and really don't have time to discuss the war with you at this time." With that, Josh turned and walked away from the old hippie and went to his office.

A week later, Josh, thinking he had seen his last patient, walked out into the lobby. Sitting there was Joe. Joe had been in one of the troops Josh had command of in Nam.

With a smile on his face, he walked over to him and shook Joe's hand. "Great to see you!"

Joe got a serious look on his face.

"Josh, I am the hippie." Josh stopped in his tracks. "You? Why?"

"It's like this, Josh. We did not kill babies. We were there to protect people's freedoms. We did not. I guess the only thing I must ask is this. Why were we really there? I think of all the men I killed. I think of all their children who will never be born. Yes, maybe I did kill babies."

Then it hit Josh. "Mourning takes on many faces. It takes everything from a direct loss to mourning losses that we inflict. The outcome is the same. We must find a way to deal with the loss. I can only imagine what an abortionist feels. He or she kills babies all day long. Does this person ever think of the generations of people they are killing in that clinic? Do they ever feel remorse for the children they have killed? If they do, how do they deal with the blood on their hands?"

Joe shook his head. "They have convinced themselves that the babies being killed are not real babies. Remember, we called the VC gooks. We did that to make them less than human. It took the guilt away from what we were doing. That's what the abortionist does by calling the baby a choice. They have made it less than human. If it's not human, there is no reason to mourn its death. A dog gets more mourning than the baby snuffed out by the abortionist. Vietnam was the beginning of this country losing its collective heart. It was the time when the country would become callous to killing. The scores of the killing on the nightly news would numb the population to the grief that each family would feel at the loss of their soldier. It's too bad that they don't keep the scores of the babies killed every day in the abortorium," Joe said as the anger welled up inside of him.

Josh got a concerned look on his face. *That would bring to reality for millions of people what this country is doing.*

At that second, a beam of light went through Joe's mind. "I've got it," he said.

"Got what?" Josh responded.

"The answer. Let's start an ad campaign. We will show mobs of people screaming at us as 'baby killers' when we came home. Let's turn it back on them. They are the same people who now claim that killing a baby in the womb is a right of a woman. We need to start showing the hypocrisy of that position. We start by showing men, in uniform, walking down a street with people shouting, 'Baby killer!' at them. Then we show one of those same women being taken into the abortion room in a clinic. I think that just may have an enormous impact," Joe answered.

"I have an idea of how we could get this whole thing kicked

off. We start with a simple call into a local radio talk show. We start to share the total hypocrisy of their position. From there, we escalate it. I am being blessed with a large income. I have always felt the thing to do is give it back. I think it's time to get aggressive with our attacks on the killers of the most innocent of all people. The abortionists who kill the children in the womb."

It was Friday morning. Josh had just gotten out of bed. He walked into the living room and turned on the radio.

"This is the Goldman on CDGE Radio in Cloverton. We are here with the best talk in town. I am here to take your calls this morning."

Josh listened for a while. The conversations went from taxes to the new school that was being considered by the school district. Josh got a slight grin as he thought, *Now's the time.* With that, he picked up the phone and called the radio station.

"This is the Goldman talking at you this mornin'. What is on your mind, my friend?"

"Good morning, Mr. Goldman. I am a Vietnam vet. The other day, I was watching the nightly news. I saw a bunch of liberal ladies protesting the newest Supreme Court judge because of his possible wanting to turn over this country's current abortion stand. Yet these are the same ladies who called us 'baby killers' when we came home from Nam. We did not kill babies in Nam, yet they are killing babies every day in the abortion butcher houses. I just think that is the height of hypocrisy."

At this point, Goldman started to stumble with his words. He was not expecting that the conversation would get this hot. "You said you are a vet. I thank you for your service. I am not sure though that they are on the same equivalency."

The anger started to well up in Josh. "How can you say that? You had the VC strapping bombs to little kids sending them at us. And you have babies being killed for convenience. Yet we are the bad guys. We were there to protect American lives. At least that was what we were told."

Goldman did not know how to handle this situation. He knew everything Josh was saying was true. He just could not figure out how to handle it. "Josh, could you hold through the commercial break?" Goldman asked.

"Sure, no problem" was the answer that Josh gave.

They broke to commercial.

"Look, Josh, you have some valid points here. I just don't know where we should go with this conversation. What points do you want to make?"

"Mr. Goldman, the point I want to make is this. The left says it cares about kids when it is convenient for them, but they are totally hypocritical about it when it comes to the life issue. The reason a baby can be killed by a liberal when it is because the baby is not convenient for them. Yet when that same baby can be seen as an asset to them, it becomes a whole different story."

"Normally, I would let it go. But for whatever reason, we have to talk about it this morning." Goldman looked at his producer and said, "Let's go."

"Folks, we are back. This is the Goldman with Josh on the phone. Go ahead with your thoughts, Josh."

"It's like this. When using children is convenient for the left, they are all for kids. But when a child is inconvenient, they kill it."

"What do you mean, 'kill it'?" Goldman asked.

"It's like this. A woman gets together with a guy, and they create a child. That child is alive from the point it is conceived. But if it is not 'convenient,' they have the right to kill it. However, when they can use children to pull at people's heartstrings to get more control of our lives or to open the borders to people who don't have a right to be here, then they will protect those children all day long," Josh answered.

"I see what you are saying. What you are saying is true. Here's the sixty-four-dollar question. What on God's green earth can we do about it?" Goldman asked.

"It's really quite simple. We must call out the hypocrisy that they are guilty of. You have to do it, and I have to do it in my profession."

The Goldman asked, "And what profession would that be?"

"I am an MD," Josh shot back.

"Again, my question. What can we do about it?" Goldman asked.

Josh walked across his office. He ran his hands through his hair. He turned and walked back. He was thinking and praying at the same time as he tried to figure out what could be done. What could be done to change the path of a great nation that was heading to a confrontation with the God of the universe for destroying the people he was creating to take care of it? Josh knew in his heart of hearts that it all had to stop. *Father, what can we do? What is your will in this? How do we stop it?* he prayed to the Father repeatedly.

Goldman spoke directly to Josh. "There must be something we can do. Children are dying every day. There must be something we can do."

Suddenly, a light went on inside Josh's head. "What did the hippies do in the sixties when we had men dying in the paddies of Nam? They did sit-ins. That's what we need to do. We on the pro-life side of the issue are too nice. On occasion, some nutcase will kill an abortion doc. But no one has gone to the point of doing sit-ins inside abortion clinics. Not only in the lobby but throughout the clinic. We will shut down the clinic for a day. No one will get hurt. Maybe some babies will be saved. Jesus said, 'Let the children come to me. Do not forbid them, for such is the kingdom of God.' If we can help save just one child that day just maybe, we can start a trend where pro-life folks start to take their job seriously. It's time to go to work."

So, it started. Josh and Goldman started to work with every pro-life association in the country. They figured out that the first thing they had to do was get people mobilized. They had to have people understand that it would be a long, hard journey but, Lord willing, a journey worth traveling.

They would encourage the sit-in tactic. They started having meetings to discuss the tactic for every butcher shop that did abortions. They discussed how to find out just what day the murders were conducted. Then covertly, they would have people spread out near the abortorium. When the doors would open, they would rush it and have people sitting in every room and every office. Every abortion bed had someone sitting on it. The baby killers were screaming at the top of their lungs for the people to get out. The people sat wherever they were in the killing chambers and smiled. For a day, they had preserved the lives of the innocent. The police were called.

Sergeant McDougal walked in. "Okay, folks. You made your point. It's time to get up and walk out of here. We don't want to arrest anybody."

Josh looked at the officer. "Sergeant, I am a doctor and a Vietnam vet. If I am not mistaken, your job is to protect life. They want to kill innocent babies here. You can try to arrest us, or you can turn and walk out and let us do the job that you won't. Let us protect the babies."

McDougal stood there, silenced. The look on his face was one of confusion. A minute went by. He turned to his men and said, "Okay, guys. Let's get out of here and let these people do their job."

As he walked out, the press was standing there, waiting for him. "What are you doing? Aren't you going to enforce the law?"

The officer looked straight into the camera. "They are protecting innocent life. I will not stop them." He turned with his men, and they walked off.

The mayor, a pro–baby killer, was incensed. "I will fire the whole police department if they do not do their job and remove those people!" she shouted from the hatred of those 'unwanted' babies. She had had a couple of abortions herself. "They were hired to do a job. Either they do it or we will find someone who will!" she again shouted.

The officer walked up to a female news reporter.

The reporter put the microphone in the officer's face and asked him, "How can you not remove those people from the clinic so the people in the clinic can do their job?"

The anger welled up inside the officer. "It's like this. You're sitting in your home. A stranger comes in with a tire iron to beat you to death. Do you want us coming into your home to stop the criminal?"

The reporter, not being used to being asked questions, just looked at the officer. "I will ask the questions, if you don't mind. And these people are not in their home."

The officer had a light go off inside his head. "No, but the babies are in their home. They were invited in. Now the mom, instead of having a few months of discomfort, would rather kill the child than give it life, even though she could give it up for adoption."

Goldman looked at Josh. "Have there ever seen sit-ins at abortion clinics? My next question is were they successful?"

Josh smiled. "I just happen to have a copy of an article from 1978. It was written in the *Washington Post*. Take a read."

With that, he pulled the article out of his briefcase that was sitting beside the desk. It read as follows.

Osenfeld

August 9, 1978

Jeanne Miller, 18, will be starting her sophomore year at Yale University this month—if she doesn't decide to go to jail. Her best friend from Bowie High School, Diane Bodner, 19, will go back to the University of Maryland—unless she too chooses being in custody over paying a $500 fine for disobeying a federal judge's order not to stage a sit-in in a Fairfax County abortion clinic.

Both young women have been arrested and jailed before. While others their age are worrying about boyfriends, clothes, or jobs, they worry about fetuses, nuclear war, lobbying legislatures, and "stopping the killing."

The two friends are part of what they claim is a growing movement of anti-abortion protestors involved in "nonviolent direct action"—the intellectual descendants, they say, of Mahatma Gandhi, Martin Luther King Jr., and the Berrigan brothers. Between 300 and 500 people, mostly young and educated, are involved in these sit-ins at abortion clinics in 15 states, according to National Right to Life Committee estimates. The committee held a workshop on nonviolent protest at its last convention.

For no discernible reason, the Washington area has been the scene of more sit-ins than any other place in the nation.

Since the country's first anti-abortion sit-in at the Sigma Reproductive Health Center in Rockville in 1975, there have been more than a dozen in the Washington area, including the six at the Northern Virginia Women's Medical Center in Fairfax, where Miller's and Bodner's latest arrests occurred.

The "pro-life" versus "pro-choice" battle promises to be a long one, waged for years to come in courts and capitol buildings as well as in frontline skirmishes such as the Fairfax incidents.

Since the U.S. Supreme Court decided in 1973 that the abortions in the first three months of pregnancy should be a question for a woman and her doctor to decide—an event commemorated in metal bracelets saying "January 22, 1973" that both Bodner and Miller wear—groups such as the 11-million-member Right to Life Committee have been trying to counter it. As the fight intensifies over questions of Medicaid funding parental permission and constitutional amendments, so do the emotions.

A "pro-choice" spokesperson said that "nonviolent" sit-ins are not nonviolent at all, that in fact, they rupture a woman's right to privacy and, as one put it, attack her "personhood" as surely as if she had been smacked in the face.

"Pro-life" militants contend that abortion is murder and have decided that the only course acceptable to their consciences is to "place our bodies between the (pregnant) women and the room where abortions are performed," as 22-year-old law student Burke Balch phrased it.

Though participants say the sit-ins grow spontaneously from discussions among members of an affinity group of pro-lifers, they are carefully organized in the sense that people are appointed to be media contacts, others to be arrested, and others to carry signs, distribute literature, or sing. Some people, called counselors, "inform the women of alternatives available to them that we love them and support them," Bodner said.

During the first part of the July 27 contempt hearing in which federal judge J. Calvitt Clarke ordered Miller and Bodner and their codefendants—David Gaetano, 27, and Mary Beth McKernan, 18—to pay the fine or go to jail for 30 days, a woman sitting in the front row got up. Pregnant and carrying an infant under one arm, she walked slowly up to the rail that separates the participants from the audience. Almost reverentially, she placed a hand on the shoulder of one of the protesters. Then she ritually touched the next. As she placed her hand on the third, a female marshal asked her to stop. She shrugged off the marshal's restraining arm. The marshal then led her firmly to the door, and she began screaming something unintelligible. She continued to scream as she left the courtroom, and her screams echoed through the closed door until she left the building.

Neither Miller nor Bodner remembers exactly when she knew she was against abortion.

"I remember hearing about the (1973) Supreme Court decision on the radio and thinking, 'Oh, that's dumb. They just legalized murder,'" said Bodner.

The two met in ninth grade gym class five years ago. Miller was a new student, and Bodner took it upon herself to make friends. She noticed Miller's metal Right to Life bracelet and asked her what it was; finding they shared views on abortion helped get the friendship started.

Miller's involvement began even earlier. She chose to live with her father in Bowie after her parents separated; her four brothers and sisters moved with her mother to Ocean City. She spent half a year in New York City when she was twelve, living with Jewish relatives and going to a Catholic school.

"My father used to take me to antiwar marches to observe," she said. "We were going to the Kenneth Clark lectures at the Smithsonian, and they were on Saturdays, like most of the marches. My father is big on education. He'd take us fossil hunting, or to see buildings torn down, to the theater . . . his whole idea was to be open to other ideas. When I was 13, I asked him for some books about abortion. He said, 'You already know you're against it. Why don't you read books on the other side?'" So she read Alan Guttmacher and Paul Ehrlich and found, she said, that reading works by these population control advocates horrified her.

"When Jeanne was in fourth grade," said Bodner, "her father sent her a letter that said, 'Today you will learn about logarithms,' and then he explained them in a way that you could really understand." For a time, Miller's father helped run the Prince George's County Right to Life chapter out of his basement. He was a stockbroker, she said.

Miller skipped the eighth and eleventh grades and then spent an extra year of high school in New Hampshire at Phillips Exeter Academy before entering Yale. She has worked as a laboratory technician in Rockville for the last three summers. During her final year at Bowie High School, Miller skipped school often to represent the pro-life position at health fairs, debates, and school classes and to lobby on Capitol Hill.

Both women reflect a seriousness of purpose that is unusual at their ages. One day in August 1974, Bodner wanted to find Miller, whom she had not seen for a while. "I figured she'd be at the Senate Subcommittee (on Constitutional Amendments) hearings," Bodner said, as though she were talking about the local fast- food teen hangout. As it happened, she looked in the newspaper to see where the subcommittee was meeting, took a bus from Bowie to the Capitol, found the hearing and her friend.

Abortion protest has taken up an increasingly large chunk of their lives as fellow protesters make up their social as well as political friends. Neither has a fixed address right now. Bodner is living with a pro- life organizer; Miller is "staying with friends" until she goes back to school. Neither is sure of anything in the future—profession, marriage, goals—other than a certainty that they will participate in more sit-ins. The way they see it, the purpose of the sit-ins is this: that while they are at the clinic, abortions are not being performed. Thus, they are "saving lives."

"It's like walking down the street and seeing a man beat up a child," Miller said in a comment echoed in almost identical words by Bodner in a later interview. "What do you do—write a letter to your congressperson and say child abuse is bad? Some laws are so unjust, they have no claim to your conscience."

The protesters compare Judge Clarke to judges in Nazi Germany who condoned the slaughter of Jews. "Everything that happened in Nazi Germany was legal," Miller said. "What we're trying to say is 'This is my brother you're trying to kill, and I'm going to try nonviolently to protect him.' So,

I'm not going to leave willingly because his life is at stake."

Not everyone agrees that their actions are nonviolent. "A lot of the women they're scaring the hell out of are there because they're very young or have a medical problem like diabetes or are carrying a terminally diseased fetus—you have no way of knowing why a woman is there just by looking at her," said Davida Perry of Washington-based Religious Coalition for Abortion Rights, an association of church groups supporting the Supreme Court decision. "It doesn't occur to them that maybe a woman who's there was raped or that they've already been through a great deal of torment. They're doing violence to her personhood. They see her as a symbol and not as an individual. That's more than I can stomach."

A 26-year-old government employee who was waiting to have an abortion when Miller, Bodner, and the others sat in at the Northern Virginia Women's Medical Center on July 20 said the demonstration was an invasion of her privacy. "If I go to the doctor for a cold, I don't expect to have a Christian scientist there in the office saying, 'Don't take pills,'" she said. "I can understand their point of view," she added. "But I don't see why they should try to impose it on other people."

"By being here, they may provoke violence," said Sharon McCann, director of the clinic. "I've had to restrain boyfriends. They get so angry at these people invading their privacy. One guy even put his feet through a glass coffee table. He was so mad."

Bodner and Miller said the parents would prefer them not to be arrested. "My parents said, 'It's your choice, but we don't have to support you,'" said Bodner, who has supported herself for a year by working as a waitress. "The thing that's hard to justify to ourselves," Miller said, "is the two and half years when we weren't doing sit-ins."

Josh smiled as he said, "You see, the violence they are worried about is not from the pro-life side. It is from their side. If you read the angry boyfriend, it makes it clear where the violence is coming from. It's the baby killers that are the violent ones. What we must do is get the pro- life folks to start getting radical again. The 'movement' has become docile. We do things quietly that change minds of some of the young ladies who have been 'duped' into thinking that is an easy way out of a position that they find themselves in."

Goldman smiled. "You know, Josh, I have always liked shaking things up. I think it's time now to start shaking up this whole movement. There are lives at stake. We need to save the babies. Let's get to work."

The two men would start the networking process. They would start to contact churches in every town. They would put posters in churches that would accentuate the need for life-saving acts that would save babies' lives. The cry started to get out over social media. It was time to go to work. The tide was about to turn. The question was which way?

*   *   *

The Battle Plans Are Made

Josh was sitting in his living room, drinking coffee with his bride. Then there was a knock at his door. It was his good friend Officer Jon Michael.

"Hey, Jon. What's going on?" Josh asked.

"Josh, I have been reading what you guys are putting on Facebook. Don't you know there is a law against trying to use social media to incite riots?" Jon said with authority.

"What riots?" Josh answered.

"The whole thing about sit-ins at abortion clinics. People will say you're trying to start something."

Josh chuckled. "My friend, we are going to save lives. We are going to attack those who would kill babies. We are going to stop the so-called doctors—I prefer butchers—who are killing the babies."

Jon sat silent for a bit and then spoke. "I am not sure this is going to work. I think what will happen is you will get some jail time. Are you sure you want to take those steps?"

Josh smiled to himself. "Ever hear the story of the guy on the shore throwing starfish back into the ocean? A person came up to them and asked what they were doing. The person throwing the starfish back said it was obvious. They were throwing the starfish back into the ocean. When asked what difference it would make, the person responded by saying that it makes a difference to the fish they throw back in. We could be saving doctors or the person who will build the next rocket that will take us to the stars and back. It matters to them."

Jon could only say, "Yup, I guess it would. But I do have to tell you this. You go into an abortion clinic; I will arrest you."

"Listen, Jon, you're a believer, right?"

Jon's response was quick. "Yeah."

"Whose law would you rather uphold? Man's law or God's?" was Josh's response.

"God's" was Jon's initial response. "But I do have a job to do, and I will do it" was the rest of his response.

"My friend, you better decide. Remember, Jesus said, 'He who is not for me is against me.' You cannot have it both ways. You are either willing to protect God's kids or not."

The look on Jon's face was priceless. "Man, you are putting me in a tough situation. I am probably going to lose my Job. When you did your first sit-in, that officer lost his job. I like my job. But I must look at who is really running this thing. God help me."

Josh spoke words of encouragement to Jon. "He will, my

friend. He will."

Jon could only say one thing. "I sure hope so. I mean, I really hope so."

Josh looked over at Jon and took a step toward him with the limp of an artificial foot. "Jon, how much is a life worth? The message we must get out is this. This country is at war. It's a civil war. That war is being waged not to free slaves. It's being waged to protect someone even more helpless. It's being waged to save the lives of preborn babies in the womb. When we were in Nam, we fought to save folks who would end up living under communism and not really care. We lost over fifty thousand men for nothing. They called us baby killers when we came home. Right now, I am willing to die for all those kids as all they really want to do is live. They want to have a chance to make a difference in this world. They are being sacrificed on the altar of convenience."

"That's a pretty bold statement you just made, my friend. But I do know you put your life on the line for those who did not care. Now you are putting your life on the line for those who just want to live. I respect you for that. But I do have to do my job," Jon responded.

"So, in this instance, your job is to protect murderers. Is that correct?" Josh snapped back.

Jon, trying to protect himself, answered, "My job is not to decide who is innocent or guilty. My job is to see what looks to be a violation of the law and stop it."

"Is it against the law to kill kids?" Josh asked.

"Yes" was all that Jon could say.

"Then do your job or stay out of the way of us who want to save children's lives." With that, Josh turned and walked away from Jon.

Jon stood there, thinking, *What just happened?* For days, he walked around with a cloud over his head. *If I let them do what they want to do with the abortion clinics, I lose my job. If I stop them, I may lose a whole lot more. God does not take kindly to people killing his kids. Lord, what do I do?* He walked across the room. He grabbed a towel that was sitting on a coffee table and threw it at the wall. He looked up to heaven and simply prayed. Father, why would you let me walk into a situation like this?

*   *   *

In heaven, his prayer was heard loud and clear.

"Peter now is the time when we get to find out just what Officer Jon is really made of. He prayed. He knows what the right thing to do is. My Spirit will speak into his spirit and turn a light on inside his mind. Babies will be saved because he listened to me. You see Judy Johnson over there? She just found out she is pregnant. The baby was conceived during an affair she was having with her doctor. She knew what she was doing was wrong. She thinks if she does not tell her husband, the problem will go away.

She loves her husband. She does not understand why she did it. My Spirit is going to communicate to her husband, Jim, that something is wrong. She is going to the abortion clinic tomorrow. There will be a sit-in going on in the clinic. She will not kill my child tomorrow," the Father said.

*   *   *

The next day, they were sitting on the counters; they were sitting in the killing rooms on the tables. The police were called. They stormed into the clinic. They asked the people to leave. The policemen looked to Jon for instructions as to what to do.

Jon looked at Josh with a pleading look on his face. "Folks, we don't want to arrest anyone. Calmly walk out of here, and no one goes to jail."

Josh got up, walked up to Jon, and went nose to nose with him. "You have a choice. Arrest the people who are trying to save God's most indefensible kids or leave us alone and let us save babies. Remember, Jesus said, 'What does it profit a man to gain the whole world and lose his soul?' The choice is yours. As for me and my family, we will serve the Lord." He walked toward the killing room, walked in, pulled out his handcuffs, and handcuffed himself to the table.

Jon walked in. "Now why did you to that?" he asked.

"Jon, you want to move me from here, you will cut off my hand. I will not let you cut the cuffs," he said, his eyes cold as steel as he looked Jon in the eye.

Officer Jon went into the waiting room. "Folks, go home. I declare this 'clinic' closed for the day. Maybe tomorrow you can have the children ripped out of you, but no abortions today."

Judy heard what Officer Jon had to say. At that moment, she realized that it was a baby inside of her womb. At that second, she decided to go home and tell her husband that she had been unfaithful and that she carried the doctor's child. She left the killing chambers in tears. She had thought she was going to "get rid of" the "problem." She walked outside of the abortion clinic, sat down on the bench outside, and cried. A prayer went through her mind. *Now what, God? Now what?*

Just then, a mother came walking by with her three-year-old son. The little boy walked up to her, took her hands in his little ones, and asked, "Ma'am, why are you crying? Jesus loves you. Give your problem to him."

Judy sat there, stunned. This little boy had just spoken the truth into her life. She realized what she had to do. She could not kill the child that she carried. She did not know where the whole thing was going to end up, but this, she did know—she had to tell her husband that she had been unfaithful and ask for his forgiveness. She had to be willing to accept the consequences of her bad decisions. She raised her head to speak to the little boy. He and his mother were gone.

That night, she would walk up to her husband. "Sweetheart, I have something to tell you. If you choose to walk out, I will understand. I had an affair."

The stunned look on her husband Jim's broke her heart. She knew deep down that she had just destroyed a man who had been totally trustworthy for the last ten years. Jim turned without saying a word and walked out the door. Judy could hear him screaming uncontrollably. She dropped to her knees in grief over what she had done. She put her hand on her abdomen. Her mind went to the child that was growing inside of her. What would she do? Just then, Jim walked back into the house.

"Sweetheart, where are we at? Do you want a divorce?" Jim asked.

"No, I don't want that. But there is one other thing that I need to tell you. I am pregnant. I went to the abortion clinic to take away my shame. God had other ideas. Pro-lifers had stormed the building. They were having a sit-in. They could not do an abortion. God the Father has a purpose for this child. He went to a lot of trouble to have me give a second thought to my decision. I choose life."

Jim put his head in his hands. He prayed silently and then out loud. "Father, what would you have me do?" He looked to heaven; he had a light hit him. "Sweetheart, I do love you. We have three kids now. We are going to soon have four. You will not tell the doctor about this child. It is mine. We will raise this child as part of the family."

The tears started to run down Judy's face. "What have I done to receive such love?"

Jim was starting to cry. "Hon, the baby did not ask to be conceived. You made choices I wish you had not made. This baby was made in sin. But here's the thing. We have all sinned and fallen short of the glory of God. I am not without sin. I may not have committed adultery, but I have sinned. We now have our fourth child on the way. Let's do this right. We will not take this child's life."

At that point, the words "Blessed are the merciful, for they shall obtain mercy" went through Jim's mind. He looked over at Judy and saw a look on her face that said it all. He knew that the love he had shared with her at that point in time had assured her fidelity for the rest of her life. Never again would they go through what they had just been through. He had shown her a love that could come only from one place: God himself.

*　　　*　　　*

Blessed Are the Poor in Spirit

Josh was sitting in his office; the nurses were coming and going. His pager went off. "Dr. Josh, your next patient is here." They showed Jake Baxter into his office.

"Jake, I have not seen you since we were in Nam. How are you?" he said as he reached out with his hand to shake Jake's.

Jake took his hand. "Josh, it's like this. Nothing has worked for me. It seems like everything I do is wrong. I have wrecked my marriage. My kids don't want to have anything to do with me. What can I do?"

Josh got a concerned look on his face. "Tell me about your relationship with Christ," he said.

"What's that?" Jake answered.

"My friend, part of the reason you're in the situation you are in is you have not been playing by the rules of the one who created you. You have been making them up as you go along. That works very seldom. We are each created for a role in God's purpose. When we have surrendered to the lordship of Jesus Christ, we can be led to accomplish that part of God's purpose we are created to do. Are you familiar with Joseph from the Old Testament?"

Jake got a really puzzled look on his face. "Nope."

"It's like this. Our Father in heaven plans by the century, not the day. He knows what the end of everything looks like. He knew that for there to be love and the people he was creating in his image, there had to be a choice not to love. To have a choice to do the right thing, there had to be a choice to do the wrong thing as well. God the Father—through his Son Jesus, by his Holy Spirit—knew that man would choose wrong. He had a choice. I thank him for the choice he made in keeping us around. Man has a way of looking inward instead of outward. We have a way of letting the enemy of our souls have our lunch. What we must be able to do is walk in what he has given us. We all have a part in his plan and purpose."

Jake got a look of disgust on his face. "Man, what are you talking about? I go through life, I survive, and I will die. That's what this life is about. Not doing things for some Santa Claus out there somewhere."

"Jake let's figure this out. If I can prove to you God exists, what will you do with that knowledge?" Josh answered.

"Then I guess I would have to accept his plan" was his answer.

"Jake, what kind of car do you drive?"

"I drive a Ford Pinto," Jake answered.

"I suppose that somehow that car just fell into place. It's a total accident," Josh stated with authority.

Jake got a quizzical look on his face. "What are you talking about?" he asked.

"Jake, it's like this. Your life is a mess. You have tried to do everything on your own. Let's look at the human body for a second. There is nothing more complex that has ever been made than the human body. Yet people say it's an accident. But if you ask a person if their car was an accident, they acknowledge it was not. Yet they say the human body, which is much more complex, was just an accident. That, my friend, does not make sense to me. I think it's time to stop trying to run your own life. On the contrary, it's time to give your life back to the person who created you. It's time for you to surrender and take your role in his purpose."

The two then parted. Jake, as they left, promised that he would consider everything that Josh had told him. They departed promising to be in contact the following week.

The next day, Josh woke up and looked at his bride, Sharon. "Sweetheart, for some reason, I have to do breakfast at McDonald's today."

Sharon shook her head. "McDonald's?" she asked. "Why?"

Josh smiled. "Not a clue, I suspect our Father in heaven has something special set up."

Sharon walked up to him and kissed him on the cheek. "Have fun, stud. Just remember who's here waiting for you."

Josh pulled Sharon close to him. "Why not come with me, sweet one? Two are better than one in some of these situations."

She smiled and threw on her jacket. "Let's go see what God has for us."

With that, they headed for their local McDonald's. They walked in, bought their meal, and found a table close to a window. Josh looked out the window. There was a young lady sitting on the sidewalk outside their window. They looked at each other and knew what they had to do. They got up and walked outside to speak with the young lady.

They would quickly learn that she had been sober for only two and a half days. They would ask her if she needed to be transported to the nearest Teen Challenge to be able to get the help she needed. Josh got on his phone and called Tim Johnson, the director of Teen Challenge. On their way to Teen Challenge, they would learn things about this young lady that would strike them to their very core. They would pray with her and then give her their numbers, telling her, if she needed to talk, to call them.

After dropping her off, they headed back to McDonald's. They would walk back inside, totally drained. They also realized that the Father—through his Son, by his Spirit—had just shown them that they would have a special ministry to people who were truly weak in spirit.

They arrived home, emotionally wiped out. In the time they had spent with the young lady, they would have their energy pulled from the deepest parts of their being. They would realize that helping a person who is truly poor in spirit would cause them to realize that they would have their energy totally sapped from them by helping that person.

Josh walked into the living room, looked out his picture window, and told Sharon, 'Babes, I realize that the Father has us on a course of dealing with people who are experiencing the beatitudes, but I just wonder how to follow up with some of these people."

Sharon smiled. "Josh, our Father has shown you people he wants us to help. He has brought them across your path. I think he is capable of putting the people in your presence who need our help. Your time with each person will be brief. He is also capable of bringing them back. Your only job is to tell these folks what the Father wants you to tell them. Nothing more, nothing less. Got it, tiger?"

Josh got quiet for a second, looked to heaven, and said, "Got it."

*   *   *

Blessed Are the Pure in Heart or Don't Touch God's Kids

Two days later, Josh was driving to his office. He looked at the sidewalk and slammed on his brakes. He saw a woman in Moslem garb being mercilessly attacked on the street. He got out, walked up to the man doing the attacking, and quickly slammed him to the pavement.

Josh, standing over him, stated emphatically, "You never lay a hand on a woman. Never."

The guy stood up. "Listen, mister. We are Moslem. My wife disobeyed me. Mohammed says I have the right to beat her! Why don't you mind your own business?" Then he stood up. "There is no god but Allah!" he yelled.

Josh looked at the woman. "Do you want to stay with this..."

She removed her covering. The woman underneath, an attractive blonde, shook her head. "Please get me out of his presence. Divorce papers will be filed today. Can you help me? My kids are in school. I will want to get them out as well."

Josh picked up his phone and called his bride, Sharon. "Babes, we are going to have a few house guests for a few days."

"What do you mean 'house guests'?" she responded.

"Tell you what—we will talk about it when I get home."

Four minutes later, Josh and Theresa drove into the driveway.

Josh walked Theresa to the door. They walked in, and Sharon got a look on her face of "Now what?" Josh would take the next few moments to explain what went on.

Sharon looked at him and asked one little question: "Do you think this could be dangerous?"

Josh responded with two words: "Could be."

Sharon got a grin on her face that he only saw occasionally. "Let's do it," she responded. "We have not had any real action for a while," she said with a look that even scared Josh.

Theresa walked over to Sharon. "Could you drive me over to the kids' school? They get out in a few moments. I do not want their father anywhere near them," she said.

"What is the problem?" Sharon asked.

"I started dating this guy in college. Everything was great. He said he had no problem with me being a Christian. That was a lie. As soon as we were married, he demanded I denounce Christ and become a Muslim. I should have divorced him then."

Sharon grabbed her keys and said, "Let's go."

They drove to the school to get the kids. As Theresa and Sharon were leaving the school, Theresa's husband drove up. One could see the anger on his face. Sharon got everyone in the car quickly and headed for their house. She got on the phone and called Josh as they were driving. Josh, having friends in high places, got on the phone to the mayor's office. He explained what was going on. The mayor had several squads two miles away from Josh's home to stop the man.

As Sharon and Theresa drove through the intersection, several squads blocked it so Theresa's husband could not follow. Omar slammed on the brakes, got out of the car, and shook his fist at Theresa and Sharon as they drove away with the kids.

The officer walked up to him and said. "Sir, if I were you, I would let the courts take care of this. You are not doing yourself any favors by showing this much anger, which we can testify to in court."

Fuming, Omar stated, "She is my wife. Those are my kids. They belong to me as much as this car does. They are for me to do what I want with them. If I am to beat my wife, it is because Allah, in the Quran, says that I should."

The officer could see all kinds of problems with this guy. He got on his cell and phoned Josh to warn him of the problems that could be coming his way. Five minutes later, Sharon and Theresa and her children arrived at their beautiful home.

Ahmad, Theresa's eldest, walked up to Theresa and asked, "Dad's not going to beat us for this, is he?"

Josh put his hand on Ahmad's shoulder. "Young man, one thing you don't have to worry about here is anyone hurting you. Believe me when I tell you this. There are few people who can stand against the hurt I can dish out when I must. I know that man can't hurt you as long as you are here."

The smile on Ahmad's face caught Josh off guard a bit. It was the smile of relief. Theresa had three children, and each child would have their own room in the twelve-bedroom home that Josh and Sharon owned.

As Josh and Sharon lay in bed that night, Sharon took Josh's hand and placed it on her tummy. "Josh Henderson, you are going to make an amazing father."

Josh sat up in bed. "You're…"

Sharon smiled. "Yes. Finally. I am about six weeks along. Promise me one thing—you will never strike our child. We both know there are ways of discipline that are not violent."

Josh smiled. "You got it, babes."

The next morning, Josh's cell went off.

"Dr. Henderson here."

"Doctor, this is Officer Jamison. We have a man here who would like to see his children. Can we bring him over?"

"Not a chance" came the quick answer from Josh. "I don't want that man anywhere near my home. You do not have my permission to give him my address. Let's arrange a meeting place," Josh answered.

They decided that they would meet at McDonald's. Mac's was extremely busy that day. Theresa's soon-to-be-ex-husband was there when they arrived.

Josh looked over at Theresa and said, "This is what we want. The more people, the better."

As Theresa's husband walked up to her, she had only one thing to say to him. "You son of a swine! Don't you ever come close to me or my children again. I am tired of the beatings in the name of Allah. He is the devil. He is Satan. The sooner you figure that out, the better it's going to be for all who are involved with you."

His face turned red with anger. Calling him a son of a swine was a huge insult. He raised his hand to strike her and had his arm immediately wrenched up behind his back.

Josh got close to his ear. "If I were you, I would just walk out and not look back," he said.

Theresa's husband turned to Theresa. "I am going to have a fatwa put on you. You better watch your back. I want my children back!" he yelled.

Josh looked directly into her husband's eyes. "You are walking on some extremely dangerous ground here. Your god uses hate and threats to control people. Our Father whom we serve is defined by his Son, Christ, with one word—*love*. On Good Friday, the Jews picked Barabbas over Jesus. That's exactly what you are doing. It's time to start to think about who you are serving. Your wife is choosing life over death. She is choosing freedom over slavery. You lied to her throughout your dating until she married you. Then you enslaved her. Now is the time to choose life over death. Jesus wants to set your family free. Please let him."

The anger her husband had was clear. "She is my wife. She is my property. Either she will come with me now or she will be killed."

Josh gave a little chuckle. "My friend, Jesus said, 'I am the way, the truth, and the life. No one comes to the Father but by him.' Allah is the father of lies. It's time to listen to the truth, receive it into your life, and be set free."

Theresa's husband stormed off, got in his car, and drove off. Theresa and her three kids got into the back of Josh's van, and they drove back to Josh's home.

Josh walked in, picked up his cell, and called the Acme Security Service. "This is Dr. Josh Henderson. Because of some things that have happened, we need twenty-four-hour security here. Please send your representative to the hospital in the morning to sign the papers."

He then called his friend, the superintendent of schools, to get the kids moved to another school. The super had a better idea. They would just have their security department work to make sure the school was always secure. If Theresa's soon-to-be-ex came on campus, he would be arrested post haste.

The next day, the kids came running down to breakfast. All were in the kitchen for breakfast. Josh would lead in the blessing of the food; the kids were feeling relieved that there would be no more beatings. They were feeling happy that they were safe, but suddenly, the eldest child, Ahmad, got a worried look on his face.

"What if Dad is at school waiting to steal us away?" he asked.

Josh smiled. "I am driving you to school, I can handle anything your dad tries to throw at us. Let's just get on with our day and not worry about it."

Relief could be seen on Ahmad's face. He relaxed and got busy with his day. They walked out to the minivan and headed to the school.

As they arrived at the school, all seemed right. Ahmad looked around and suddenly realized that there were policemen all over the place.

Ahmad looked at Josh and asked him a question. "What are all these policemen doing here?"

Josh smiled. "It's nice to have friends in high places. I am talking about the Lord Jesus Christ first and the officials of this city second. You see, my young friend, the police have a report of what your father tried to do to you. Your mother filed a complaint when he tried to attack her. She also warned that your father thinks beating children is his God-given right. The judge is placing a restraining order against your father, forcing him to stop. I think they are hoping he shows up here so that they can arrest him. Child abuse is not an acceptable thing in this area of the county."

With that, the kids hopped out of the car and went into the school for a full day of study. Josh turned the car out into the street and headed to his office to spend the day seeing patients. As he sat down in his office, his phone rang.

"Dr. Henderson, phone call."

He reached over and took the call. "Dr. Henderson here. May I help you?"

"Dr. Henderson, this is the principal of Jefferson Elementary School. The kids' father is here tearing the place apart. We have called the police. Would you be willing to take some time from your day to come over here just in case someone gets hurt? We have an ambulance on site. But I think you could bring a great deal of peace to the situation," the principal said.

Josh looked at his calendar. He realized his patient load was full that day. He had people who needed him coming to his office. He also had kids at the school who needed him. He faced a real dilemma. Then it hit him—Ted Johnson. Ted was an old friend who was a retired doc.

He got on the phone. "Ted, I have a problem. Could you get over to Jefferson School? They have a guy going nuts over there. He is a Moslem who wants to enslave his children into that religion. He lied to their mother to get her to marry him. Then the abuse started. Now he is attacking the school to try to get his kids.

It's time for it all to stop. Can you get over there in case someone gets hurt? They have an ambulance on site. I just think having a doc there would help."

Dr. Ted, drinking his first cup of coffee of the day, said, "I am on my way, Josh. Been a while since I was in a combat zone. Let's see what I can do to help. I am taking my cell phone with me. I will call you if I need your expert advice."

Dr. Ted drove up to the school. There were several police cars and an ambulance on site. It appeared that no student were hurt and the children's father was being led out in handcuffs. Dr. Ted grabbed his cell and called Josh and filled him in on what was going on.

Smiling, Josh said, "Ted, thanks for being there. Check with his kids and make sure they are okay. Tell them I asked you to come. I am busy with patients and cannot get away. Remind them that God the Father—through his Son Jesus, by his Spirit—has their back."

Dr. Ted went to the school office and told the principal who he was and that Josh had sent him. He then asked that the children be told that he was there. As the children walked into the office, Ted could see the looks of concern on their faces.

Dr. Ted smiled. "Josh could not make it. He has an office full of patients. He sent me to make sure all was okay. How are you doing?"

The kids smiled and told the doc they were okay. Dr. Ted then told them that Jesus had their back and how great a friend Josh was to them.

Ahmad spoke up. "Dr. Josh saved us from a terrible situation. Now he makes sure people are here to help when we need it. Thank you, Dr. Ted, for being there when we needed you."

Ted smiled as he put his hand on Ahmad's shoulder. "My pleasure, son. My pleasure."

The smile on Ahmad's face was as broad as the sea. The joy of feeling protected from beatings was not comprehendible.

The relief on Theresa's face was priceless. Knowing her children were being protected from the beating of a man who was so engulfed by a false religion that it took over his whole being was something rare in this day and time. What she was not able to understand was why anyone would be so wrapped up in a hateful belief system that would destroy anyone who would not bow to its hateful practices.

The children's "father" then decided to rush the building. He pulled out a gun and rushed the building. That was a huge mistake. The police had stationed sharpshooters on the parameters of the building and on the roof. One shot, and he was on the ground. The sharpshooter had been careful not to make a deadly shot but to place a bullet in his leg to drop him to the ground. Another officer rushed forward and kicked his gun away.

His hands were cuffed in front of him. He was loaded into the ambulance, and two officers climbed in as well to protect the med staff on board. He would be rushed to the hospital, where more police staff would be there to read him his rights. He would have a public defender waiting there for him to protect those rights. Dr. Ted hopped in the ambulance with the kids' father.

He looked at him as he said, "Those children are my property. You have no right to take them from me. Allah gave them to me, and no one can take them away. I will die trying to get my kids back."

"Well, sir, I think you will be spending a few years in prison for what you did. When you get out, your kids will not be children anymore but will be Jesus-loving adults who will not be threatened by the likes of you," Dr. Ted stated with authority.

The anger on the kids' father's face could not be hidden. As the ambulance pulled up to the door, the staff was there to help unload the wounded man. They quickly wheeled him into the ER. He would be rushed to surgery, where they would remove the bullet from his leg. When he awoke a few hours later, his attorney was standing beside his bed.

His attorney was blunt. "Sir, I would suggest you cut a deal, if you can. This goes to trial, you could spend the rest of your life or close to it in prison. They have you on camera rushing the school with a loaded gun. That carries a life sentence. You can cut a deal, maybe, and get out in thirty or forty years."

The kids' father looked at his attorney. "You mean I may never see my children again?" he asked. "I wish they had killed me," he continued.

His attorney looked at him, smiled, and said, "My friend, that, would have made you a martyr. The government is careful not to do that. Remember the mastermind of 9/11. He confessed, hoping to be put to death. He got life imprisonment in solitary confinement. My job is to defend you. So, we must find a way to justify what you did. They have you recorded rushing the school with a gun. That recording is going to be on the nightly newscasts all over the country. We cannot erase that scene from people's minds. So, sir, what is the justification we can use to show that your actions were reasonable?" his attorney asked.

"Those are my children in that school. They don't belong to their mother. They belong to me. I would have you know that Allah gave them to me as my property."

This statement ticked his attorney, Sam Smith, off. "Sir, when does that ownership end?" he asked.

"When my children marry. With the girls, their new husbands own them. With the boy, he would take ownership of his wife and any children they may have," the children's father said.

Smith had thoughts going through his mind. *If I get this guy off, he will raise hell for those kids and could possibly murder his wife. If it is clear I have thrown the case, he has grounds for appeal.* He then turned toward the kids' father. "Sir, to be honest, the case they have against you is pretty tight. I can try to defend you, and I will give you the best defense I can, but if I were you, I would take a deal if the prosecution is willing to give you one."

The kids' father looked at Smith. "What crimes could they convict me of? Wanting my children back with me?"

Sam shook his head. "How about having a loaded gun near a school? You're lucky that a cop did not simply take you out." A thought went through his mind. *I wish they would have.*

"How long do I go away for?" he asked.

"Ten to twenty is my guess," Smith answered.

"They are going to send me away for wanting my family back," he said.

"No, they, the court, would be sending you away because you are a threat to not only your children but to every child that was near them," Sam answered.

"And what happens if we don't get a deal?" he asked.

"Then we go to trial. If we lose, and chances, are we will—you are probably looking at thirty years."

"Is there any chance of getting off?" the kids' father asked.

"I am good, but to be honest, the evidence is overwhelming," Sam answered.

"Make the deal," he said.

Sam called the DA. "Fred, what kind of deal are we willing to give this guy? How generous are you feeling?"

Fred Smith, the county attorney, shook his head. "Sam, to be honest, he did not hurt anyone. The only thing we have him on is the gun in a school zone. He did strike a police officer. We can add that into the mix. I think this guy is a loose cannon that someday will hurt someone. But we can't put him away for something he might do. Let's offer him three to five years. By law, that's about the best we are going to be able to sustain. If he were to appeal anything other than that, we would get blown away."

Sam knew he had to keep his opinion out of this. He just kept his mouth shut and went back to the kids' father. "We have a deal. They are offering a three- to five-year sentence with the possibility of parole. I think it's the best we can do. What do you think?" Sam asked.

"Let's go talk to the judge" was his answer.

*   *   *

The county attorney, Sam, and the kids' dad were in the judge's chambers.

The judge looked at the deal. "There's only one thing that I am going to add to this. You will never see your kids again until they are eighteen and old enough to decide. I will sentence you to twenty-five years, stayed for three to five assuming you do not go near any kids. You stay away from all schools, and you never own a gun again. Is that clear?" the judge said.

"And if I decide I want a trial?" the kids' dad asked.

"You better hope you get off. Because if you don't, I will send you away for the rest of your life," the judge answered.

"I'll guess I'll take it," the kids' father stated.

The guards came in, cuffed him, and took him back to his cell. Thoughts were going through his mind that he did not dare express to anyone in the room. He did not want to give any reason for appeal.

Sam looked at the DA. "I guess you will be calling Dr. Ted to pass on the news," Sam stated.

"I already have. He told me the kids were grateful that their father will not be hurting them anymore. But it was clear, even though he was totally brutal to them, they still loved him. They hurt for him and that his actions ended up with him going to prison. I think that when they become adults, they will be able to have some sort of relationship with him." The DA looked at Sam. "The power of love will never cease to amaze me. A father can brutalize his children. They still love him. Somehow, I can't help thinking that he loves them. But it's like they can't comprehend what love really is."

Sam looked at his friend, the DA. "I think what some of these dads need is a lesson on how the author of love defines it—1 Corinthians 13, if you will. 'If I speak in the tongues of men and of angels but have not love, I am a noisy gong or a clanging cymbal. And if I have a prophetic power and understand all mysteries and all knowledge and if I have all faith so as to remove mountains but have not love, I am nothing. If I give away all I have and if I deliver up my body to be burned but have not love, I gain nothing. Love is patient and kind. Love does not envy or boast. It is not arrogant or rude. It does not insist on its own way. It is not irritable or resentful. It does not rejoice at wrongdoing but rejoices with the truth. Love bears all things, believes all things, hopes all things, endures all things. Love never ends. As for prophecies, they will pass away. As for tongues, they will cease. As for knowledge, it will pass away. For we know in part, and we prophesy in part, but when the perfect comes, the partial will pass away. When I was a child, I spoke like a child, I thought like a child, I reasoned like a child. When I became a man, I gave up childish ways. For now, we see in a mirror dimly but then face to face. Now I know in part. Then I shall know fully, even as I have been fully known. So now faith, hope, and love abide, these three, but the greatest of these is love.' The key verse is this. 'When I became a man, I put away childish ways.' Men don't throw temper tantrums. Men know how to discipline their children with love. That discipline is not one that causes the child to fear the father. But it is what causes the child to respect the position of the father as father."

Josh walked into the courtroom with Theresa and their

children. Their father walked in with Sam and took a seat at their table. Judge Gus Hendrickson walked in. He looked over the courtroom and saw all the people sitting at their tables.

As he walked in, the bailiff gave the cry. "All rise!"

All in the courtroom rose.

"You may be seated."

All in the courtroom did.

Judge Hendrickson took his seat. "Would the defendant please come forward?"

The children's father came forward and stood with Sam at the judge's bench.

The judge looked at the children's father and asked him, "How do you plead?"

The children's father wanted to plead "not guilty." He knew if he did, there would be no chance of him ever seeing his children again. "Your Honor, I plead guilty and throw myself at the mercy of the court." The judge got a frown on his face. "I read the report. Do you really think your god Allah gives children to you as a piece of property like a car or a house?"

The children's father answered quickly and with confidence. "Those children belong to me, as does their mother. When we married, she became mine to do with as I pleased. When the children were born, they became mine as well. You can put me in prison, but you cannot take the ownership of the children away from me."

The judge frowned as he said, "I hereby sentence you to twenty-five years in prison. You are eligible for parole in three to five years. You will have no contact with the children until they have reached the age of majority. Which, in this state, is eighteen. Mister, you step out of line or have any contact with the children, and you won't see the light of day for twenty-five years. Is that clear?"

"It's clear" was the only answer he dared to give.

The children's father asked the judge if he could at least hug his children and say goodbye. The judge allowed them into his chambers to do so. The children were crying, as was their father. The children knew that what was happening was for their protection, but they still loved their father. The love went deep. The father felt he was being persecuted for being Muslim. What he would find out was the United States protected kids. He would also find out prison justice could be quick and brutal. He would also find out his tenure in the prison would be short. The children would soon be fatherless.

When the children heard what had happened to their father in prison, their emotions exploded. They screamed and shouted and cried. Their father had beaten them and their mother, but he was still their father. They had a love for him. They realized that their lives would be different. They both had a sense that their Father in heaven—through his Son Jesus, by his Holy Spirit—had a plan for them to take part in his purpose. Their father would not even let the name of Jesus be spoken in their house, but they realized that everything had changed. They just had to get used to what the Father was going to set up for them.

Theresa just sat and prayed. "Father, we have to get into a good church. Please direct us to where you want us to be. Amen."

The next day, they were driving down the street. They drove by a little church, looked at the sign, and saw "First Church." Theresa got hit with a flash of light. She and her two children walked inside. The young pastor walked out of his office, greeted her with a smile, and welcomed her and her children into his office.

"I am Pastor Jim, and who might you be?" he asked.

"I am Theresa. I am sure you have seen in the news the stories of my late ex-husband. I was raised in the church. I want to get back to it," she said.

"Theresa, let me ask you a question. Being part of a church is great, but if you have not received Christ as your personal lord and savior, it is not quite there. Have you received Christ?"

She just sat there and thought for a moment. "No, I don't believe I have. Can you help me with that?" she asked.

The children spoke up. "Can we accept Christ as well?" they asked.

Jim smiled. "You sure can. Please pray after me. Father in heaven, please forgive us of all our sins, and, Jesus, please lead us in the ways of salvation and use us to bring other people to you as well. And, Lord, please fill us with your Holy Spirit. In Jesus's name. Amen."

When the children and Theresa finished praying, their expressions of joy filled their hearts. They were so overjoyed that they could hardly keep from jumping all over.

Then Ahmad stopped in his tracks; tears started to come to his eyes. "If Dad would have received Christ, he would probably be with us today."

Jim got a sullen look on his face. "What happened?" he asked Theresa.

Theresa did not want to go into details at this point. "He was killed in prison. Can we leave it at that for now?" Theresa said.

Jim smiled. "Of course," was all he had to say.

Dinner was amazing. The children were immediately drawn to Jim.

Then the look on Ahmad's face changed. "Mr. Jim, are you going to be like our dad was? He believed we were simply his property. Something to be used and abused for his pleasure. How can we trust that your God is any better than Allah?" Ahmad asked.

"Ahmad, it's like this. I try to live by the Bible, which is the word of the living God, who is the great 'I Am.' He sent his Son Jesus that we could be saved from all our sins. God the Father loves all kids and does not want them hurt or punished unjustly. In the book of Luke, Jesus said, 'Let the children come to me. Do not forbid them, for such is the kingdom of God.' You can find that in Luke 18:16. God loves his kids. You prayed and received Christ. You are his kids. God the Father will wipe out anyone who hurts kids. If the Father sees fit to put your mom and me together in marriage, I will be your protector. I promise you this. If you mess up and there must be consequences for your actions, I will never hurt you. You may lose a cell phone or get grounded or write a hundred times 'I will do this or that.' I will never strike you."

The two kids both smiled.

"That, I think we can live with," the young lady said.

*   *   *

Blessed Are the Pure in Heart

It was the Fourth of July weekend. Josh and Sharon were walking on the beach beside the Gulf of Mexico in Florida. As they walked along, they came across two lost children. They looked to be twins, about five years old. They were crying, but the glow on them was an amazing thing to behold.

"Kids, where's your mommy and daddy?" Josh asked as he looked to the right and the left.

The little boy in tears looked at Josh and said, "A man grabbed us, told us he had candy for us, and started to run down the beach. When you showed up, he ran off."

As they stood there beside the children, Josh saw a man and woman looking frantic down the beach. He started to wave at them. As they approached, the children got up and ran to their mom and dad.

Josh walked up to the dad as the little boy was telling them what happened. "Sir, I am Dr. Josh. I have a practice downtown. If you would like to bring them in, I will check them over for you, no charge. There are a lot of nutcases out here. Your kids are a precious gift from the Father through his Son Jesus, by his Holy Spirit. You must keep a better eye on them."

Their dad, Abe, looked at Josh. "Thank you for being there. These kids are nothing but energy. They don't quit. But their

119

exuberance can get them in trouble. I am considering putting them on those leashes that attach to their backs."

Josh smiled. "You know what? Sometimes that little bit of restraint is needed. At the age of two, at age five maybe."

"I just wish I could have gotten my hands on them," Abe said.

Josh only half-smiled as he said, "No, you don't, my friend. You stop them, and then you turn them over to the police. Your violence against them will leave your twins fatherless. That would not be a good thing. The best thing you can do is let the Father take care of it. I will guarantee his justice is more final and more memorable than yours ever will be."

Just then, they looked to the east. They saw a man slinking away from where they were standing. They realized that the culprit was trying to slink away. Josh, being in top shape and quick as Greased Lightning, was on him, quick as that. He had him tackled and on the ground. Both the twins ran up and said that he was the guy who had tried to steal them from their parents.

At that second, Abe had a choice to make—let his justice rain down on the guy or let the police take care of it, and the guy would spend years and years behind bars. His mind went wild. *How could I take this guy out and get away with it?* He thought. This guy had tried to grab his kids. God only knew what he would have done to him, yet he was the one who would do jail time if he touched the scum. He looked to heaven and prayed. *Father in heaven, what about that? How is it that I would be the bad guy for taking this guy out if he was going to hurt your kids?*

Just out of his vision, almost covered by a veil, he seemed to hear a voice. "My son, remember when my Son Jesus was talking to the people standing around him. He said to them, 'It would be better for a millstone to be tied around their neck and be thrown into the sea than to cause one of these little ones to stumble.' You see, my child, it would be better if he had never been born. His death on this earth will be prolonged and painful, and when he hits hell, that pain will last forever."

Abe looked around himself. He thought he knew that it was the great 'I Am' who was speaking to him. He looked at the shell of a man being cuffed by the police, and he could not help but smile. He really wanted to go up to him and say something like "Enjoy your stay in hell, pervert." At that point, he knew he should not. He wanted to do it, but he did not. Instead, he walked over to him and looked him directly in the eye.

"I will tell you this. The time you have left on this earth is not going to be pleasant for you, but your eternity can be different. If you repent, if you let the Father—through his Son Jesus, by his Holy Spirit—touch your life and change you from the inside out, if you are willing to be used in prison, then your eternity can be saved. If you are not willing, then your eternity will be one of pain that you could not experience on this earth, and that pain won't go away." Abe turned and walked away.

The man who had tried to steal his children turned white with fear.

Josh and Abe walked to the cafeteria and sat with the two kids. They had malts, and the two men drank coffee.

Abe looked at Josh and asked a question. "Josh, do you think I was too hard on that creep?"

Josh looked at him with a profoundly serious look on his face. "Look at your kids. They are five years old. Their hearts are pure, and the Father, in his word, states, 'Blessed are the pure in heart. For they shall see God.' Your kids have that purity glow on them. That glow is part of what makes them so attractive. That glow is what draws both good and bad people to them. I have seen people who have not lost that glow. It's amazing. One can tell that their heart truly is pure. Abe, do whatever it takes to communicate to them, as they get older, the importance of keeping that purity all through their lives."

Abe's eyes became moist with tears. One could see his lower lip start to quiver. He looked at Josh and asked him how one could do that. Deep in his soul, he was feeling totally inadequate.

Josh looked at him and smiled. "There is also a verse that says, 'With God, all things are possible.' Rely on the Holy Spirit to keep you focused on how he wants you to accomplish those things. Remember this—he will never leave you or forsake you."

Abe smiled.

His kids ran up to him, smiling widely. "Daddy, please let us sit on your lap and just snuggle," they asked.

Abe pulled them up onto his lap. He could feel them cuddling up to him.

The warmth of their unconditional love was totally evident to Josh. Josh's mind went back to Ahmad and his sister as they hugged their dad for the last time. He had beaten them, and he had abused them, yet they still loved him. When they found out about his demise in prison, they cried. "You see, part of the reason God loves kids the way he does is most are not jaded yet. They love with his love until they are taught to do otherwise."

*   *   *

Blessed Are You When People Speak Evil Against You Falsely

Judy knew her limitations. She loved working with children, and she loved doing things for children. Her occupation was such that she got to work with them daily. Because of this, an organization in town wanted her to take over the treasurer's job and buy gifts for the kids using the credit card of the organization. She told them she did not want the job. She explained to them that her organizational skills left much to be desired, and she knew that her lack of said skills would get her into all kinds of trouble. The problem she ran into was they were so insistent that she finally gave in to the pressure. You see, they knew her to be a goody-two-shoes, and they wanted to hang her out to dry. They wanted to put her into a position where she would make a mistake and they could use said mistake to wipe her out.

It started during the Christmas season of 2018. She was sent out by the nonprofit to buy Christmas gifts for the kids who did not have anything under the tree. They gave her the company credit card and told her to go to work. She had a wonderful time, knowing that the lives that her Father in heaven would touch through her would be many. Many lives were touched that Christmas. Her biggest problem was her lack of organization. She forgot to turn in the credit card receipts. As a matter of fact, she lost them.

John Stinkberry, the CEO of the organization, called Judy into his office. "Judy, do you have the receipts for all those gifts you purchased for the children that we have in our storeroom for the kids for Christmas?"

Judy turned white. "Mr. Stinkberry, I will look and see if I can find them."

She hurriedly started looking all over the office. Her mind was racing as she was frantic. She looked for two hours and could not find the receipts. She had to find them; she knew if she did not, she would probably lose the job that she really did not want in the first place for fear that something like this would happen.

She walked back into his office, knowing she would be in a whole lot of hot water. "Mr. Stinkberry, I am afraid I have no idea where those receipts would be."

Mr. Stinkberry was not amused. "Judy, did you not realize just how important those receipts would be to this organization? There is no way of us knowing how many of those gifts you could have kept for yourself. I must take action that I really don't want to take. I am afraid I have to call the police," he said.

The next day, Mr. Stinkberry had an appointment with his doctor. He went simply by Dr. Josh. Stinkberry walked into Josh's office with a rash on his arm that would not go away.

Josh looked at him and asked a question. "What's going on in your life that causes stress right now? I can find nothing physical that could be causing this rash."

Stinkberry looked at Josh and proceeded to tell him about having Judy arrested for misappropriation of funds.

Josh got an interesting look on his face, halfway between just being curious and disgusted. "Tell me a little about this young lady," he said.

Stinkberry proceeded to go into detail about Judy, her strong points but also her weaknesses and disorganization.

Now this really ticked off Dr. Josh. "What you're telling me is this. She turned down the job three times. You almost forced her into it. Then she messes up, and you put her in jail?" Then Josh really lost it, using words he used very little. "Stinkberry, what kind of ass—— are you? Get out of my office now. I will be calling downtown to get this fixed. There is no way that young lady should be in jail!" he said, raising his voice. "You coerce her into a job she knew she should not be in. Then when she messes up, you put her in jail?' What kind of businessman are you? She had no business being in that position!"

Stinkberry got red in the face. "All right, what are you going to do about it?" he asked.

"I have friends in high places. I am also going to take this to the press and blow it up big time. This will make your business look really bad in the public eye," Josh answered.

126

Stinkberry was getting angrier and angrier. He knew the nonprofit could not sustain that kind of negative press. He could see only one way out. That was to quietly drop the charges.

"Josh, I have always respected you. How could you take the side of this loser? You know as well as I do that, she probably packed her basement with some of that stuff she was supposed to give to the kids."

The anger went through Josh like a bolt of lightning. "How dare you malign a child of the king? She knew she should not be in that job. You guys set her up for failure. All she ever wanted to do was to help the nonprofit. Yet you just wanted a scapegoat for its failure. You really should be ashamed of yourself."

Stinkberry knew Josh was right. He also knew he could not admit it. He knew that to fight this thing out would be futile. "Look, Mr. Henderson, you think being a high and mighty doctor gives you special power to know what's right and what's wrong. She broke the law and has to pay the price like any of us would."

"Mr. Stinkberry, let me put it this way. She asked you how many times not to be put in that job. Yet you told her it would be all right. Then when she messes up, you want to put her in jail. How much of a bum are you?"

The anger could be seen in Stinkberry's face. He did not like his character being called into question for anything, especially not for him wanting to throw the sweet Judy to the wolves and putting her in a cage for years. The evil that was inside him had him convinced of his righteousness.

Josh walked up to him and smiled. "Stinkberry, remember this. Jesus came that we could have life. The expense for us to have that life has been paid. You want to take away some of that life from the young lady named Judy. You know as well as I do that, she was set up by you for failure. So here is my idea. I think it will help both parties. Judy must learn to be careful with all the responsibilities that are put in front of her. Many times, in life, we are given things to take care of that we really don't want to deal with. Nevertheless, we must take care of what is put in front of us. I propose this—that Judy be required to make up for the lost funds. You could set up a payment plan to accomplish the reimbursement. That way, your business gets what is coming to it, and Judy learns a lesson in taking care of what she is put in a position to take care of."

"Josh, I think you may have something there. If we do that, she learns a lesson, and the company does not take shots for attacking a young lady who screwed up. She messed up not with a spirit of malice, but she was trying to help. Let's do it."

The plan was set to make the situation right. They presented the plan to Judy.

The anger started to well up inside of Judy. "Listen here, Mr. Stinkberry, you are the one who told me to take your company card and buy the stuff for the kids for Christmas. All you had to do is look at your statement. You have one purchase made at Walmart for $5,000. That's what you say you are short. You had the gifts that went to the kids. Granted, I should have taken better care of where that receipt ended up. But there are other things that can be done to track them. I really don't feel I owe you anything," she said with a look of total disgust on her face.

Stinkberry picked up his phone, called his accountant, and had him look at his e-bank report from that period. There was a purchase made for the $5,000 from Walmart. They had had a toy distribution of $5,000 worth of toys for tots. The redness on his face could have started a big campfire. He looked at Judy and started to apologize. He turned to his office manager and told her to write a $1,200 check to Judy for compensation for his error. Then he told her to find Judy another job with the organization that did not have handling money involved with it.

His next step was to pull Josh aside. "Josh, can we not have this go to the press? If it does, it could really have an adverse effect on what we are doing here."

Josh looked Stinkberry right in the eye. "I still should go to the press, but I do see you as being one who does a lot of good for the community. To be honest, I wonder how they got a guy like you to head this organization. I am sure you must have some redeeming qualities to you. Could you tell me what you have in mind for this little girl?"

Stinkberry nodded. "We are creating a position for her to be a liaison to the young people of this community. So many times, judgments are made that should not be made before all the facts come in. It could be how a person looks, or it could be how they talk or how they walk or how they dress. What Judy is going to do is to start sitting down with young people and start to work through some of those problems. As she does that, hopefully, the young people will start to think about what they are doing and how it affects their future. I think that will be a position for which she is well suited."

When Judy heard the news, she was elated. Then came even better news. All the charges had been dropped. Her sigh of relief could be heard around the world. Josh was standing near her. She ran up and threw her arms around Josh in such a huge state of gratitude. As she hugged him, she started to cry.

Josh looked at her and asked, "Judy, are you sure you want to keep working for this guy? He has shown himself to be not really trustworthy. Something happens, he will come after you again."

As Josh walked across the room, a holy bolt of lightning struck him. "I have got it." He picked up the phone and called the head of the nonprofit. "Kevin, Josh Henderson here. You have a problem that about cost the nonprofit a lot of money and reputation. It had to do with a young lady by the name of Judy who was put in a position that she was not cut out for. Your guy Stinkberry, when she messed up, had her arrested. We got everything worked out, but it was not without the promise of going to the press to plead her situation. My fear is this. To cover his incompetence, he may pull that stunt on someone else."

Kevin listened to what Josh had to say. Kevin then asked Josh who he thought would be a good manager of the day-to-day with the nonprofit.

"I think Tom Morris would be an excellent manager, if he would take the job," he answered.

With that, Kevin had his secretary get ahold of Tom Morris. Tom had managed some huge nonprofits in the past and enjoyed the process. When Kevin got in touch with him and explained the situation, he was more than willing to take on the project to make it work. Kevin then made a call to Stinkberry and informed him that his services would no longer be needed and that they had found someone they thought would be better in that position.

When Kevin walked in and talked to Judy, he found out that this young lady had some great ideas for how they should be reaching kids. She also informed him that recordkeeping was not one of her strong points. She asked him if he understood what had happened with Stinkberry, and he answered in the affirmative. He also told her that he was in the past, and from that point forward, they would have as their only objective to make the kids that the

Lord brought in as functional as possible in society, and they would be a great witness for Christ in all that they did. This would allow Judy to work for several more years reaching kids. There would be generations of kids who would be made into functional adults because of Judy's service.

*   *   *

Blessed Are the Peacemakers

Steve Jameson woke up early to the phone beside his bed ringing off the hook. He picked it up. Groggily, he answered, "Jameson here. What can I do for you? A shooting? Going on now? People going to the hospital. I'll be right there."

Julie, his wife, looked over at him. "Sweetheart, what is it?" she asked.

"A shooting at the mall. Lots of people hurt. There is a doc on the scene who was shopping at the time. They need all hands-on deck for this one."

As he drove up to the mall area, he noticed a familiar face, Josh Henderson. Josh spotted Steve in a second. They ran up to each other.

Josh looked at Steve and said, "Steve, they got the perp. He is cornered, but we have a whole lot of people wounded. The one good thing is no fatalities."

Just then, an officer ran up to Steve. "We have him cornered in a restroom. Do we have permission to take him out?" the officer asked with fearful excitement in his voice.

Steven put his hand on the officer's shoulder. "Let me talk to him. There has been enough bloodshed for one day. If I can talk him out of there, then maybe we can figure out why he did what he did. Nothing justifies the spilling of innocent blood, but let's see what I can do."

As Josh was pulled away, treating victims of the shooting, saving multiple lives, Steven would be standing outside a washroom door, talking the shooter into giving up his weapon.

Josh was to find out the guy really did not want to hurt anyone. There were a lot of leg wounds but nothing life-threatening. Josh was scratching his head. *What was this guy trying to prove? He comes in here, shoots the place up, and then locks himself in a restroom to try to save himself— or maybe get himself killed?*

Steven would spend the next hour talking to the guy in a calming voice. He did not want the guy to commit suicide; he wanted to find out what was going on inside the guy's head. The only way of doing that would be to get him to walk out and put his gun down.

"Okay, Mr. Steve, I am going to open this door slightly and slide the gun out. After that, I am going to walk out with my hands in the air. Is that going to work?"

Steve gave a sigh of relief. "Please slide the gun out now," he said.

The man did as he was told. The door opened slightly; the gun slid out on the floor.

Steve then said, "When you come out, make sure your hands are above your head. If you start to reach toward your pockets, you will be taken out. Is that understood?"

"Yes, sir, it is."

The next thing that happened was the door would open every so slowly, and the man would walk with his hands in the air. He would be put in handcuffs immediately and removed from the mall area and head to the police department for questioning. Josh and Steve met after, and Josh thanked Steve for being the peacemaker that he was in that instance.

"Steve, we are all given gifts. The gifts you have, I don't, but there is one thing I am coming to understand. The peacemaker can make peace in several different ways. One can be to bring peace to an argument between siblings. Another is what you did today. My friend, you helped me understand another beatitude today. 'Blessed are the peacemakers, for they shall be called the sons of God.' My friend, how does it feel to be called a son of God?"

Steve smiled. "Pretty good. No, I mean really, really good. No deaths. I feel really good."

As he started to jump up and down with joy over a job well done, Steve started to walk away. The sun was shining, the breeze softly brushing away the leaves that were lying on the ground. As he turned the corner, he heard tires screeching as some young people were driving totally out of control and crashed into the side of the Carpenters State Bank. He heard children screaming. He grabbed his cell phone and quickly hit speed dial and called Josh to get over to the bank.

Josh hopped in his car and put the pedal to the metal and arrived at the bank in record time. As he got out of his car, the ambulances were pulling up. He ran over and checked on one of the crash victims and saw a huge gash on her head.

"Help me," she said weakly.

She had been standing on the corner when the car screamed around the corner. She stepped back as they rammed into the side of the building, knocking the awnings off, and some bricks came loose. One of the bricks fell from the third story and hit her directly on the top of her head, knocking her to the ground. She shook her head as she stumbled to the ground. As she lay there, she was having trouble staying awake. She knew that she had taken a hard hit on the head. She knew she had to stay awake.

Josh knew how important it was to keep her awake as well. Steve started to direct traffic until other policemen who were specialists in traffic control arrived. People were panicking, and Steve knew the importance of trying to bring some tranquility to the bad situation. He heard the sirens as police and an ambulance were on the way.

Steve heard a child crying, an infant. He looked around the corner and saw a young mother holding her baby tightly. He walked up to the young lady and asked what was wrong. The young lady held up her arm to show a huge gash and blood flowing all over the place. Steve took the baby in his arms and called for

Josh on the double. Josh took one look at the injury, picked up his radio, and called the ambulance staff over to take care of her.

"Where is the baby's father?" Steve asked.

"I am afraid that he is working out of town all week. Is it possible for her to ride in the ambulance with us?" she asked.

Steve grabbed his cell phone and called his wife, Julie. "Jules, we need your help down here. There is a sweet young lady with her baby. We need to get her to an ER for some stitches in her arm. Could you come down, throw a child seat in the back of the car, and follow us to the ER?"

"Absolutely" was Julie's quick answer.

Josh got the bleeding stopped with a compression bandage. At the same time, Julie drove up. Steve had the child in his arms and hopped in beside Julie.

The mom with the sliced arm climbed into the back. "Let someone with a more serious injury ride in the ambulance. That way, I can be with my baby as well."

Julie drove to the hospital, following all the speed laws. As they arrived, they were able to get everyone into the ER without incident. The mother would get a couple of stitches put in her arm. She thanked both Steve and Josh for the help in the situation.

"By the way, did they get the crazy guy in the car who just about got everyone killed?" the mom asked.

Steve smiled. "The guy's gas pedal got stuck. After his crash, the car rested against the building that got so many people hurt. He was an older guy, stone sober. Just had a malfunction in his brand-new car. The crux of the thing is it was his dream car. He had wanted a new Dodge Challenger ever since he was a kid. Just like life, he finally gets what he wants, and it blows up in his face."

The mom chuckled. "Wow! Now I really feel sorry for that guy as well. What's going to happen to him?" she asked.

Steve said, "It's not really his fault, but this, I do know, Chrysler Corp is going to have a huge lawsuit, maybe a couple, on their hands. First is from the older gentleman. Second is going to be from the building owner and the city for all the damage caused from the new car. God only knows where all this could end up, and at this point, he's not telling anyone."

Steve then proceeded to help Josh and the drivers and attendants work with all the injured that one car out of control could cause. They worked at keeping the people calm until more help could arise. That day, they really found out the value of being one of the blessed—the peacekeepers.

*   *   *

Situation 1

A week later, Josh woke up on a Saturday morning, looked at his beautiful bride Sharon, and sat up and kissed her on the forehead. She moved a bit; he then traced the bridge of her nose with his finger.

She opened her eyes. "Good morning, sweetheart," she said as she smiled.

"Hon, I think I know where our Father wants me to go with this. I think it has to be a ministry of the beatitudes. I think it must be a ministry of reaching people in the situations that they are in. It does not really matter whether they are veterans or not. People all have junk thrown at them, and the body of Christ must be there to help. I do feel a call to help the veterans. Veterans Helping Veterans through Christ, I think, is what I am going to call this organization. The question is this—how do I organize this ministry? How do I set this up to be an outreach for the kingdom that will help other men going through their own beatitudes?"

The next morning, Josh awoke to his phone going off. He picked up the phone.

"Lieutenant Josh, Jay Johnson here. Can we meet for coffee?" Jay asked.

"Jay, where are you? What's going on?" Josh replied.

"Lieutenant Josh, it's like this. I have tried to get several things going in my life. Every time I do, I seem to mess up. I have crashed a marriage to the most wonderful lady in the world, I just can't seem to get anything right. What can I do?" he stated as he started to cry.

"Jay, where are you?" Josh responded.

"Right downtown. I also heard Bruce Johnson was a huge help to you. Any chance of getting him there as well?" Jay answered.

"How about tomorrow noon at the Buckle?" he asked.

"That would be great. Can you get ahold of Bruce?"

"Hold on just a second, Jay. Let me get in touch with him. I will be right back," Josh said. Josh hung up with Jay and gave Bruce a quick call.

"Josh, we can't wait until tomorrow to meet with Jay. I will be there today at noon."

Josh confirmed that time at the Buckle and called Jay back to confirm with him. "Jay, Josh here. Today at noon at the Buckle will work."

"Josh, I can't tell you how grateful I am that you will be able to meet with me," Jay said.

Three hours later, Josh drove up to the Buckle. He saw Bruce's car and saw a young man get out of his older, beat-up car.

He walked up to the young man and asked, "Are you Jay?"

Jay smiled. "I am. You must be Bruce," he answered.

"That would be me," Bruce answered. "Let's get inside, where we can talk."

Bruce and Josh sat on one side of the table and Jay on the other.

Bruce looked directly into Jay's eyes and said, "Jay, Josh tells me life has been tough for you. I bet it feels like you're living out your own beatitude."

Jay got a curious look on his face. "Beatitude?" he asked.

Bruce smiled and gave a little wink. "The beatitudes can be found in the fifth chapter of Matthew. My guess is that you could be hit by at least two of them. One would be 'Blessed are those who mourn.' You are in mourning because of some of the bad choices you have made in your life. And the second is 'Blessed are the poor in spirit.' The results of the bad choices you have made have you down. Is that a surprisingly good assessment?"

Jay looked at the two of them. "I guess Josh shared with you where I am at," Jay said.

"Pretty much. I asked him what was going on with you. He told me what you told him," Bruce answered. "You see, the beatitudes describe man's human predicament in just about any situation. What gets a person into said predicaments is different for every individual. But the crux of the situations is this, how does one get through whatever situation that they find themselves in?"

Jay's facial expression was one of a person who was totally defeated in life. "Mr. Bruce, all I ever seem to do in my life is mess up. Life does nothing but beat me down. I don't know what to do. Seems like the harder I try to get things right, the worse I mess up. What can I do? I am at the point of being ready to give up."

Bruce got a smile on his face. "My friend, you are in a place with your life where God the Father, through his Son, by his Spirit can really start to move in you. You are living out a beatitude. 'Blessed are the poor in spirit, for such is the kingdom of God.' You are at the spot in your life where the Holy Spirit of God himself, by his Son Jesus, can really start to work in your life. All you must do is surrender to the lordship of Jesus Christ, and you will start to see your life turned around."

Jay, with tears in his eyes, started to let go and really cry. "I was wondering if it was possible for anyone to love me," he said.

Bruce put his hand on Jay's shoulder. "Man, you know that people love you. You must have family around someplace. Brothers, sisters, cousins—you got to have someone someplace," Bruce answered.

"Family, sure. But don't they have to love you?" Jay answered.

"Nope, but, Jay, do you have a relationship with the living Christ?" Josh asked.

"Who?" was Jay's answer.

"Christ Jesus," Bruce responded.

"I know who he is. But to say I know him or have a relationship with him, not so much," Jay answered.

Bruce smiled. "Jay, if you were to surrender to Christ, he would change your world. He would change you from the inside out. Are you ready to have your life changed?" he asked.

Jay was smiling from ear to ear. "What must I do to be saved?" he asked.

Josh spoke. "To be saved, one must surrender to the living Christ. When you have done that, then you will feel the Holy Spirit of God himself indwell you. Once that happens and you make that final surrender, Christ will lead you the rest of your life. The changes in your life will amaze those around you but especially yourself."

Jay looked directly into Josh's eyes. "Will you help me get that relationship with Christ?" he asked.

"Jay, it starts with a prayer of surrender and commitment. Shall I pray with you?" Josh asked.

"Please" was Jay's response.

Josh then led Jay in that prayer that would start Jay on the road to a life sold out to Christ. Jay's life would turn around in ways that amazed everyone. Even Samantha, his former wife, took notice. The two of them would spend the next couple of years putting their relationship back together in Christ. Samantha had trouble at first accepting the fact that God had really changed Jay; she was not in a big hurry to deal with a person again who had all the problems that Jay had. However, as she saw the changes daily in his life, she was pulled into the relationship by Christ, which changed her as well.

*   *   *

Situation 2

Josh and Sharon were sitting at breakfast on a Saturday morning at the Buckle. They looked out the window and saw a young preteen lady being seduced by a man who looked to be a pimp. Sharon spotted the situation first and pointed it out to Josh.

"I'll be back in a moment, sweetheart." He rose from the table they were at and walked outside. As he approached the young lady and the pimp, he asked her a question. "Young lady, is this guy giving you a problem?"

The man, who was trying to put the young lady into his "stable," looked at Josh and said, "Mind your own business. I have this situation totally under my control."

Josh looked at the man and then the young lady. "Again, young lady, do you know this man?"

"No!" came her answer. "He is trying to get me to go with him."

Josh had a concerned look on his face. "Is that something you want to do?" Josh asked.

"*No!*" was her answer.

The pimp got very angry very quickly. "If you don't leave right now, you may not be able to at all."

Josh gave a bit of a chuckle. "Mister, I have led men into combat. I have killed the enemy with my bare hands. I really don't think you want to tangle with me. I would suggest that you turn and walk away. If not, you may find yourself getting hurt in areas you did not even know you had. Then when the police show up, it's going to be the word of a dirty pimp versus Dr. Josh Henderson, who is me. You may find yourself going away for an awfully long time. And believe me, the place they would send you would not be very 'comfortable.'"

The pimp did not listen to a word Josh had told him. He was under the impression that Josh was not telling him the truth about his abilities. He made a move to try to take Josh out. He got behind him and grabbed him by the throat. Josh moved quickly and had the man's arm twisted around his back, with his hand placed between his shoulder blades. The pimp was screaming like a baby in pain. Josh then twisted his hand harder and, at the same time, dislocated the man's shoulder.

Sharon was sitting inside the Buckle, watching everything through the window. She grabbed her cell and immediately called the police.

John Marshall, the officer taking 911 calls that day, took the call. "This is 911 emergency. How can I help you?"

"This is Sharon Henderson, Dr. Josh Henderson's wife. We are at the Buckle. There was a…what looked to be a pimp trying to put a young lady into his service. Josh stopped it. It looks as if he caused some damage to the individual. Would you send a squad over?"

She heard a chuckle in the background. "Josh is being a hero again. I have heard of his exploits, being at the right place at the right time. He is at it again."

Then Sharon heard the call go out for a squad to show up at the Buckle. In less than two minutes, the squad pulled into the parking lot of the Buckle.

Officer Jonsmith walked over and looked at the scummy guy lying on the ground. "Josh, what did you do to this guy and why?" Jonsmith asked.

The sweet young lady spoke up. "Officer, this man wanted me to 'work' for him. He went on and on about how much money I would make providing 'service' to the men he brought to me. I did not want to do it. He kept pushing me. Just then, Dr. Josh came out and told the man to leave me alone. When the man attacked Dr. Josh, Dr. Josh took the man apart."

Officer Jonsmith then grabbed his radio and called for an ambulance. "Young lady, are you willing to testify to that in court?" the officer asked.

Just then, her parents drove up. Her father immediately recognized Josh.

"Josh, how are you? I hear you rescued my daughter. Hope you did not kill the guy. I want a shot at him myself," the young lady's dad said.

At about that time, an ambulance showed up. Another squad was following it. They loaded the bad guy and hauled him off to the hospital, where he would have his shoulder fixed before they sent him to the county jail and court. Josh looked at the young lady and asked her to tell him about herself.

"Dr. Josh, I want to do nothing but help people. So, when he approached me, my natural inclination was to trust him. What I want to do with my life is just love people. I want to be able to trust people, but I am learning there are some not-so-nice people out there. How do I do that?" she asked.

"Young lady, we are told to be as wise as serpents and harmless as doves. In the fifth chapter of Matthew, one will find the beatitudes. Jesus laid them out for us. You seem to fit one. The one you seem to fit is the one that says, 'Blessed are the pure in heart, for they shall see God.' My dear young one, your heart is pure. I would encourage you to learn the word of God. I would also encourage you to spend a great deal of time with your father as well as your Father in heaven. Learn his word. As you do this, you will find yourself becoming closer and closer to him," Josh said.

She looked at her daddy, and her daddy looked at her. There were tears flowing from both of their eyes. They both realized just how close to a total disaster they had come.

Josh walked over to them, put his hand on her dad's shoulder, and smiled. "Dad, my name is Josh Henderson. I really feel like I was placed here because of your daughter's pure heart. In the fifth chapter of Matthew, Jesus tells us that the one with a pure heart will be blessed. They will see the kingdom of God." He looked at Meghan, the young lady, and said, "Young lady, you were protected because of your pure heart. But Jesus is standing beside you, waiting for you to totally surrender to him. He protected you because of the love he has for you."

Meghan looked at Josh and smiled. "Mr. Josh, I surrendered to Jesus a long time ago. When that man first came to me, the Holy Spirit prompted me to walk away. I did not." She looked to heaven. "Father, forgive me. I am sorry I did not listen to you. I know you want to protect me because of the heart you have given me. Please watch over me."

Josh was standing beside her when he got nailed by the Holy Spirit. "Young lady, I think I have a message for you. He protected you this time. When you get a warning such as that, listen to it. Remember this. Our Father's protection comes through obedience. He sees your pure heart. He wants to protect you. But he can only go as far as you are willing to be in subjection to him. You give off purity. Every deadbeat around wants to destroy that. He has given you that pure heart for a reason. Pray and listen."

Just then, Bruce walked in. "Hey, what's happening here?" he asked.

Josh would spend the next ten minutes explaining everything

———

149

that had just gone on.

Bruce looked at Meghan and smiled. As he smiled, he asked her a question. "Young lady, how much do you need our Father's—through his Son Jesus, by his Holy Spirit—protection?"

Tears were still running down her cheeks. "A lot" was all she could say.

"Then, young lady, I suggest you move when the Spirit touches you and warns you to move. I can see purity all over you. Don't blow it by making a mistake that you should not be making. Our Father warned Noah to go to Nineveh. He did not. He ended up in the belly of a whale for three days. What you would have gotten into if the Father had not sent Josh to rescue you would have been a lot worse. The Father loves you a lot. That's why he sent his Son Jesus over two thousand years ago. Young lady, when the Spirit of God himself speaks to you, listen!" he said with extreme intensity.

Meghan looked at her dad.

"Young lady don't ever—I mean ever—put yourself into a situation like that again. Your purity is what attracts guys like that to you. You have something they never will have, yet they see it, they want it. It does not matter—they will try to steal it from you. If they steal it from you, they still won't have it. Satan wants to use guys like him to destroy God's perfect gift. Purity. Don't let anyone take it."

By this time, Meghan was sobbing uncontrollably.

Sharon walked up to her, put her arms around her, and held her tightly. "It's okay, baby. Let it out. Sometimes our Father in heaven will use tough love to get us to where he needs us to be. Where he needs you to be is in his arms and your dad's as well. Remember this. God our Father is our daddy. He sent his Son Jesus to redeem us. He sends his Holy Spirit to protect us. Sometimes from ourselves, sometimes from cruds who would hurt us. Sweetheart, it's all right to cry. It's all right to let things out. But remember this. The Holy Spirit is always there to protect us. But we must listen to what he is telling us to be protected," Sharon spoke into Meghan's ear.

At that point, a police officer drove up. "Is there a young lady by the name of Meghan here?" he asked.

"Officer, that's me," Meghan responded. "What can I do for you?"

Officer Jones looked her in the eye. "Meghan, we have been trying to bust that pimp for years. After Dr. Josh here took him out, he confessed to everything. He did not want to face the justice that would have come his way, which we promised would. When he comes before the judge, he is going to be put away for a long time. But, young lady, be glad that Josh protected you. He would have killed you."

Once again, the tears started to flow from Meghan's eyes. She looked to heaven and mouthed the words "Thank you."

What she did not realize was that to send him to prison, she would have to testify in court about what he had tried to do to her. The pimp was hoping she would not. She was delighted to testify and put the bum away, but his attorney had plans to make the young lady look like a cheap hooker who was looking for a job.

*   *   *

God the Father in heaven decided that would not happen. He looked at Gabriel and sent him down to have a "conversation" with the pimp's attorney.

That night, the attorney for the pimp was asleep on his king-sized bed in the massive home that he lived in. He felt a bright light as he slept, which caused him to wake up. He looked up and saw Gabriel in his full glory. The lights of God were streaming off him. The attorney had to rub his eyes. He thought he was dreaming.

"Who are you?" he asked Gabe.

Gabriel, having a bit of a sense of humor, replied, "Who do you think I am?"

By this time, the attorney was so scared, he stuttered, "I have no idea. God?"

"Not at all. I am Gabriel. I have a message from you directly from the Father of all mankind. You cause that little girl, whom he loves, any trouble tomorrow in court, and your client will not be the only one who suffers for the rest of his life. You will suffer as well," Gabe stated in a voice that would scare the toughest man.

The attorney fell to his knees. He cried like a baby. Fear totally engulfed him. He realized at that second that he had better handle the young lady who would be on the stand the next day with kid gloves. He also knew that to rake her over the coals like he had planned was an awfully bad idea. He would have that confirmed to him the next day in court.

*　　*　　*

As they walked into court the next day, he spotted the young lady walking into the courthouse with Josh on one side and Bruce on the other. He realized at that second that the Father had this planned out. He realized two uncomfortable truths. One, he had to do everything he could to protect his client, and two, if he hurt this precious child of the King, he would pay for it for the rest of his life. He looked to heaven. *Father, help me*, he prayed.

The evidence that the state put forth on the pimp was overwhelming. The attorney realized he had to accomplish something that would provide justice for the young lady and protect his client. He also realized that the evidence and the eyewitnesses of both Bruce and Josh would be totally damning to any defense he tried to put forward. He could see only one way to really help his client. He had to try to plea it down.

He leaned over to the pimp. "I would suggest we try to see

what kind of deal we can make. They have way too much evidence against you. They have eyewitnesses that place you trying to persuade the young lady there that she should go to 'work' for you. If we take this to trial, you will lose, and you will go away for a much longer time."

The pimp looked over at the young lady. He could sense the purity streaming from her.

Then Gabriel spoke into the pimp's ear. "Listen to me. If you let the Father—through his Son Jesus, by his Spirit touch—your heart and you get sent away for a short period and you go in with the idea that you want to get to know Jesus Christ as your lord and savior, the Father will protect you in prison. No harm will come to you. Read everything you can get your hands on to build yourself up in Christ. Then when you walk out, you will truly be a free man. At that point, the Father will use you in ways that will protect young ladies from the scum of the earth. He will use you to take the bums who are destroying the Father's kids and start to stop their use of his most precious children. If not, you won't last a week in prison. The choice is yours."

The pimp looked around himself. No one was there. He looked down on the bench he was sitting on. There was one phrase on a piece of paper: "The choice is yours." He knew at that point his life had to change.

He looked to heaven and said one quiet little sentence: "You have a deal."

The pimp's attorney made a deal with the court for the pimp— five years, eligible for parole in two—and the pimp pled guilty and asked the judge if he could say something to the young lady. The judge looked over at her, and she nodded.

The pimp stood up and looked directly at her. "Miss, what I tried to do to you is unforgivable, but I am asking for that forgiveness. I make you this promise. When I get out of prison, I am going to go to work for some organization that is working to stop the abuse of young ladies by the men whose only goal is to destroy a young lady's purity and have them drawn into prostitution. I am also going to work hard to get to know Jesus Christ in a very intimate way."

The young lady asked the judge if she would walk over to the pimp. He nodded.

She walked up to him and asked him one question. "May I pray for you?"

"Of course," came his quick answer.

"May I put my hand on your shoulder?" she asked.

"Yes."

The young lady then placed her hand on his shoulder. "Father, I lift this man to you. Please use him where you are taking him. Teach him about your love and kindness. Teach him that the purity you build into people is for the reason of touching those you bring across their path. Use him to be that vehicle of love and compassion that you have created him to be. Father, please protect him where he is going. Use him to be that carrier of your word and your love to the people you will have him ministering to in prison. Don't let him compromise on that which is right but help him be that tool of yours to break even the coldest heart in prison. In Jesus's name. Amen."

*   *   *

After the young lady's prayer, he was to find himself in handcuffs, being hauled off to the penitentiary in the next town. As he approached the pen, he could see the white, stone-cold walls of the prison. He knew God the Father, through his Son Jesus, would be using him on the inside. He just was not real anxious to spend a couple of years at the least inside them, but he knew he had it coming.

As he walked into the prison, he looked at the faces of the men he would be spending the next couple of years with. All he could see was hopelessness. He knew these men needed to find the hope that he had just experienced through his encounter with the young lady he had tried to destroy. The pimp realized that his encounter with the little girl had changed his life, but he was wondering how many lives would be changed because he had surrendered to Christ as he went into prison.

The first person he would meet would be a man named John

Culbertson. He was serving time for assault and battery. He was a short termer. He had only six months left on his sentence. As the pimp walked in, the Holy Spirit of God himself nudged him. He could hear soft words in his ears.

"I want to touch John," the Holy Spirit whispered to him. Jake nodded imperceptibly. He knew that he had to take time to build a relationship with this man, and then when the time was right, he would tell him about how Christ got ahold of him. He would tell him that getting caught not only saved the purity of the young lady he was attempting to "recruit" but also saved him from an eternity of hell. He pointed out that all men have sinned—it does not matter what the sin is, but all men have sinned. All men deserve hell, but the sacrifice that Christ made on the cross saved men from the pits of hell and the eternal, never-ending destruction that would come with it. Time after time, he would share that truth with the men in prison. Time after time, they would repent.

By having the pimp getting caught, God the Father—through his Son, by his Holy Spirit—would accomplish a couple of things. One was to save the little girl who was pure in heart and save Jake and, through Kevin, hundreds of men in the prison system in the years that he was incarcerated.

*   *   *

Meghan, the young lady, walked away from the courthouse and looked to heaven. She felt a warmth after praying for Jake that she had not experienced before in her life. She realized that the excitement she was feeling could be a direction-giving experience. As she stepped out through the entrance of the courthouse, Josh and Bruce did at the same time.

She looked at Josh. "Mr. Josh, after praying for Jake, inside, I felt a rush like I have never felt before. I don't know what all this means. It's like God is giving me directions in what he wants me to do with my life. Do you think that is a possibility?"

Josh smiled. "Young lady, I think what happened in the courtroom was huge. In the Gospel of Matthew Jesus said, 'Blessed are the pure in heart, for they shall see God.' I think you got a glimpse of how God the Father—through his Son Jesus, by his Holy Spirit, works. I have a hunch that that prayer will be answered in a huge way. You may not see the answer for years to come. But I have a sense that somehow, in some way, you will find out."

It took five years. Jake had led over a hundred men to the throne of grace, yet he knew that one person who really needed to hear what Jesus Christ had completed in men's hearts while he was in prison was that young lady he had tried to destroy. She had prayed for him just before he was hauled off to prison. He knew that he had to get in touch with her somehow. He had one problem: he had a lifetime restraining order keeping him away from her. He called his attorney who had been assigned to him back when he went to trial. He also put a request in for Kevin Derusha, the prosecutor on the case.

"This is Kevin Derusha. May I help you?" he asked.

"Mr. Derusha, this is Jake Tommerun. Remember you sent me to prison about five years ago. I know I cannot contact the young lady I tried to recruit into my 'stable.' But I need to get a word to her. Would you pass on to her that because of her prayer in the courtroom, Christ touched me? Because of him touching me, I have been used by him to see hundreds of men's lives changed in prison. I am not going to give you my cell number. If she wants you to get ahold of me, you will have to call me back. If she wants to contact me, please tell her that she had a huge influence on my life . . . I really feel that the Father—through the Son, by the Holy Spirit—does not ever want me to have direct contact with the young lady. I am a dark spot in her life, and she must be able to walk in God's light the rest of her life," Jake said.

Derusha got a look on his face that just said, "What am I hearing?" "Okay, I will get that message to her. I am going to add something to your message. What St. Paul wrote in Romans 8:28. 'All things work together for the good, for those who are called love God and are called to his purpose.'"

Jake smiled as he said, "Perfect. I am just overjoyed that Dr. Josh was there to stop me. Please pass on to her that our Father in heaven is changing lives all over the place because of what happened."

Derusha called Meghan and asked her to meet him for coffee. They met at the Buckle instead. As he walked in, he saw the radiance that streamed from Meghan. He was taken aback by her absolute purity and radiant beauty. Her blue eyes and blonde hair seemed to light up the room. He could tell that the Holy Spirit indwelt this young lady in a strong way. He walked up to her and held out his hand. She took it, and he shook it gently.

"Young lady let's have a seat," Derusha said.

They walked over to the table overlooking the lake and sat across from each other.

"Young lady, the influence of one prayer you have prayed has brought hundreds to Christ already, and the future looks like it could be many, many more," he said.

"What prayer was that?" Meghan said with a question in her voice.

"Remember a court case a few years ago? It seems that Jake, the guy you prayed for before he went to prison, got a touch from the Holy Spirit in a big way the day you prayed for him. It compounded when he got into prison. God the Father—through his Son Jesus, by his Holy spirit—worked in him in a way no one expected. He started to minister to people in prison. He was responsible for hundreds upon hundreds of inmates coming to Christ. I had coffee with him. He is really a changed man. He wanted me to thank you for praying for him. It changed his life," Derusha said.

"I suppose he would like to talk to me," she said.

"Nope. In fact, he told me to pass this information on to you as a thank-you for the prayer. He has forbidden me from giving you, his number. He says that was a dark part in your life, and he did not think it would be wise. Besides, he knows to have any direct contact with you could land him back in prison. Breaking parole, you know."

The next day, Derusha met with Jake.

"Jake, she was excited to hear that you worked to bring so many men to Christ. She also agreed with you that she should not have any direct contact with you. She said that she was excited to see our Father working through you the way he is. But she realizes, as you do, that your paths should never meet."

Jake looked at Derusha. "At least tell her this. I am sorry, and I repent for the damage I have done to her. I also ask for her forgiveness," he said.

Derusha picked up his cell and texted Meghan just what Jake had asked him to send. She did send her acceptance of his request, and her forgiveness was sent back.

*　　*　　*

The Street Fight

It was a hot summer day. Josh and Bruce were walking toward the Buckle for coffee. As they walked past an alley, they heard yelling and screaming going on in the alley. They turned and saw two thugs trying to rob a young boy of the little money he had. They hustled down the side street and grabbed the guys and threw them up against a wall.

Josh got really close to the big guy's ear and said in an intense sort of voice, "Hey, thug, want to try me? I killed forty men in Nam with my bare hands. If you are insistent, we can make you the forty-first."

The big guy looked at Josh and Bruce and held up his hand. "Mister, I don't want anything to do with you."

He reached into his pocket and gave the young boy his money back. As a matter of fact, he gave the boy back more than he took. Both the men ran off.

Eric, the young boy, looked at Josh and Bruce. "Thanks, guys. Could you walk me home? My mom is home sick and had me run to the market to help her with some ice cream for her sore throat. These guys jumped me and tried to take the money Mom had given me for the ice cream. Can you walk me home? It's only a couple of blocks."

Both men were more than happy to help the young lad out.

First, they had to stop by the Main Street market and get the ice cream for his mom. When they arrived, they found out that she had more than just a sore throat. She told her son that so he would not worry. Bruce and Josh would find out, when Eric went to his room, that Mom had cancer and did not want Eric to know just yet. Bruce looked at Josh, who smiled.

Bruce pulled Josh aside. "What are you smiling about?" he asked. Josh, still smiling, said quietly. "It's time for a miracle."

Bruce got a concerned look on his face. "What?"

"A miracle," he repeated. "I really feel like our Father in heaven wants to heal this woman. He wants us to lay hands on her and pray."

Josh and Bruce walked up to Joyce and asked her if they could pray for her.

She gave them a puzzled look and said, "Sure. It could not hurt."

They asked if they could put their hands on her shoulders. She agreed. With that, they prayed the Holy Spirit into her heart, from her heart out to the rest of her being. They prayed that the Holy Spirit would cleanse every organ of the cancer that was trying to take away Eric's mom from him. The men looked at her for a moment. Her total countenance changed. Her face brightened up. Her breathing got easier. She threw the blankets off, grabbed her robe, and got out of bed. She looked twenty years younger.

"Ma'am, I suggest you do what Jesus told people to do after he healed them. He would send them to the high priests to confirm the healing," Bruce said.

"I will set that appointment tomorrow. I think my doctor is going to be blown away."

Eric walked into the room. "Mom, is that you? I have not seen you look, well, that pretty ever. What has just happened?" Eric asked.

"Eric, these men just prayed for me. You see, Mommy was sick. These men asked God to heal me in Jesus's name, and he healed me. I have never felt this good in my life. I am going to the doctor and have him confirm it," she said.

Eric's eyes became as big as saucers. His mouth dropped open. "Mom, I did not even know you were sick. I just thought that you were tired all the time."

She smiled at her son and then looked at Josh and Bruce. "Gentlemen, I can't thank you enough. First, you rescue my son. Then you lay hands on me and ask God the Father—through his Son Jesus, by his Holy Spirit—to heal me, and he does. I don't know how to thank you."

Josh spoke up. "Ma'am, the only one that you need to thank is the Lord Jesus Christ. He healed you. All we did was ask. We have no special powers. We just asked."

Bruce walked over to Eric. "Young man, I think the Father

had us at the right place and the right time to not only protect you but also bring health back to your beautiful mom. Now it's your turn to really be that man of the house, and, Mom, it's time for you to be honest with your son. It's imperative that you level with him about things that will eventually affect his life."

Josh looked at her. "Joyce, why don't you be in my office tomorrow at 9:00 a.m.? We have some of the best doctors around. We will run a battery of tests so we can give you the all-clear. Then you can go on with the rest of your life."

Joyce smiled at Josh and Bruce. "How can I ever thank you guys?"

Bruce and Josh looked at each other and shrugged.

"Joyce, it's like we mentioned a few moments ago. We don't need thanks. Jesus Christ is whom you should be thanking. Remember this. By his stripes, we are healed. He paid the price for all the good that happens to us," Bruce said.

At that point, Eric came running into the room. "Daddy's home! Daddy's home!" he yelled with an extremely excited voice. His smile was huge. "Daddy, these men saved me from a bully who was trying to take my money, and these guys stopped him. Then they came home and prayed for Mom, and she was healed!"

Todd, her husband, had been overseas as he was an officer in the army. "Well, gentlemen, I am not much of a believer. Seeing some things, I have seen makes me wonder where or if God is there at all," he said.

Josh and Bruce looked directly at Todd.

Josh started. "Todd, what do you do in the army?"

Todd got a look of pride on his face as he said, "I am a field operations officer in Iraq. Have either of you men been in the service?"

Josh looked directly into Todd's eyes. "I was a platoon lieutenant during Vietnam. Believe me. I have seen some things that were horrible. But this, I do know. God, my Fatherthrough his Son Jesus, by his Holy Spiritwas there with me the whole time. Even when my leg was blown off in the rice paddy, he was with me. I met my beautiful bride, Sharon, when I was in the hospital recuperating. For the woman Jesus brought to me, I would go through it all over again. We must remember Romans 8:28. 'He works all things for the good to those who love him and are called according to his name.' It's not a good thing that I lost my leg in the war, but the good he worked from it is amazing."

Todd looked at Josh and Bruce. Then he looked at Joyce. "Hon, you look amazing. Do you think you are really healed?"

"Todd, I have not felt this great in years. I know Jesus would send people that he would heal to the high priest to have them confirm it. Josh here is a doctor. I will be going to his office in the morning. He is going to have them run a bunch of tests to confirm the healing. But I feel great."

"Todd, remember this. We were at the exact spot and the exact time to be able to rescue your son from those deadbeats that were trying to rob him. He then asked that we come home with him as he was worried about those guys. Things like this don't happen by accident," Bruce said.

*   *   *

That night, as Todd slept, suddenly, his room lit up. He sat up straight on his bed. Gabriel was standing at the foot of their bed. He looked over at Joyce; she was snoring.

"Me being here won't wake her up. I am here to talk to you. You and I both know that your reenlistment is coming up quickly. Your son is eight years old. He needs his dad home. The Father, because of what Christ did on the cross, sent his Holy Spirit to heal your bride when Josh and Bruce prayed and asked him to do it. Now are you going to follow the Father's suggestion, or are you not?" Gabriel asked.

*   *   *

The next day, she was in Josh's office. He would have her get to the best oncologist in town and have her healing confirmed. She was put through a battery of tests to confirm that her healing was complete.

Mark Johnson, the best cancer doc in town, came into Josh's office, smiling. "Joyce, there is no cancer at all. It does not look like you have ever had it. What made you think you had cancer?"

Josh tapped Mark on the shoulder. "Mark, here is the file on her. Complete with the biopsy results. What happened? Last night, we rescued her son Eric from some thugs in an alley downtown. We then escorted him home. We would find out his mom was sick, and he had been sent to the store to pick a few things up. When we got him home and spoke to his mom, we would find out the extent of her illness. As you can see from her file, the cancer was quite extensive. We laid hands on her and prayed. Then God the Father—through his Son Jesus, by his Holy Spirit, did his stuff. God's healing of her has been confirmed."

Mark shrugged as he said, "Yes, she has, my friends. Yes, she has."

At that point, Todd was flabbergasted. He did not know what to say, or for that matter, he did not know if he should say anything.

Gabe, standing next to him, had only one more thing to ask him. "Are you going to follow what God wants, or are you going to do things your way? The Father protected your son. He healed your bride. Are you going to serve him or not? What you need to do is repent and ask Christ to be your lord and savior. Heavy on the 'lord' part."

Todd shook his head. He again looked at Joyce, got on his knees, and started repenting. He surrendered to Christ and asked him to be his lord and savior. Todd would serve Christ for the rest of his days. His son, Eric, would be raised and become a mighty servant of Christ the King.

*　　*　　*

Josh and Bruce were riding home.

Bruce looked at Josh. "Hey, bro, you have spent the last few years helping people get through their beatitudes. How are you doing with all the junk that showed up in your life?" Bruce asked.

"What junk?" Josh said as he smiled. I just want to keep being used by the Father to touch people every day."

*　　*　　*

At the end of the day, Josh and Bruce would go back to the Buckle before Bruce would leave in the morning to fly home.

"Bruce, I have to thank you. The Holy Spirit gave you the words for me two years ago in this very restaurant. He has brought people across my path who have been living out their beatitudes. I have come to the conclusion through this whole thing. We are all living out our beatitudes. It does not really matter which ones we are living out. We are living them out. The thing we must all keep in mind is this. What can we do to help other people get through theirs?"

"As I look back on the rice paddy in Nam, each of those men was living out one beatitude or another. Many of them would see God quickly because of what happened there. Because of what happened there, survivors were put into beatitudes they were not expecting to be in. It's our job to help them all get through theirs. But we also have to be aware that we have to work to get through ours."

Bruce looked at Josh across the table. "My brother, we have seen a lot over the last few years. We have come to understand what it really means to be used by God the Father and guided by his Holy Spirit. We should pray right now and recommit ourselves to the task that the Father—through his Son Jesus, by his Spirit—leads us into so that we can become the tool that he will use to accomplish his greatness."

Bruce reached out with his hand. Josh took it so it looked like they were shaking hands. Both men would commit the rest of their lives to listening for the Holy Spirit to lead them in ways that would allow them to be a tool used in the Father's hand to touch the lives of people as they go through their own beatitudes.

*   *   *

<u>Epilogue</u>

What beatitude are you going through? Have you had a great loss in your life that you are in mourning for, or are you the person who hungers and thirsts after righteousness? It could be any one of them.

The thing to do is to commit yourself to the Lord Jesus Christ and allow him to lead you with whatever you are blessed with in the big scheme of things. We are each called to something. That something is the beatitude in which we are blessed to be going through. Don't back down but accomplish whatever God the Father—through his Son, by His Spirit—is leading you to accomplish. Remember this. We can do all things through Christ, who gives us strength.

Be blessed.

Michael D. Goldsmith

Made in the USA
Monee, IL
23 October 2023

45087330R00098